Columbia Savings and Loan Association
is very pleased to share with you
this limited edition of *Bergen County:
A Pictorial History.* We believe
this handsomely designed and
meticulously documented volume
not only will be welcomed as a valuable
addition to your library, but also
will become a collector's item
in the years ahead.

We greatly appreciate the community
support and trust that have been
placed in us. In the spirit of continuing
and expanding that support and trust,
we dedicate this book to all who have
helped make Bergen County a unique
and special place to live.

COLUMBIA AND LOAN ASSOCIATION SAVINGS

Bergen County:
A PICTORIAL HISTORY

by Catharine M. Fogarty,
John E. O'Connor, and Charles F. Cummings

Design by
Paula Hennigan Phillips

The Donning Company/Publishers
Norfolk/Virginia Beach

Copyright © 1985 by Catharine M. Fogarty, John E. O'Connor and
Charles F. Cummings

All rights reserved, including the right to reproduce this
work in any form whatsoever without permission in
writing from the publishers, except for brief passages in
connection with a review. For information, write:
The Donning Company/Publishers
5659 Virginia Beach Boulevard
Norfolk, Virginia 23502

Edited by Richard A. Horwege

Library of Congress Cataloging-in-Publication Data

Fogarty, Catharine M.
  Bergen County: a pictorial history.

  Bibliography: p.
  Includes index.
    1. Bergen County (N.J.)—History—Pictorial works.
  2. Bergen County (N.J.)—Description and travel—Views.
I. O'Connor, John E. II. Cummings, Charles F.
III. Title.
F142.B4F64   1985   974.9′21   85-20539
ISBN 0-89865-430-0 (special edition)
ISBN 0-89865-431-9 (pbk.)

Printed in the United States of America

Contents

Acknowledgments

The authors wish to acknowledge the following individuals who have offered generous assistance in the research and preparation of this volume: Frederick W. Bogert, T. Robins Brown, Reginald McMahon, Craig Mitchell, Raymond Ralph, and Claire K. Tholl. We have also profited from the cooperation of borough historians: Robert Patton, Old Tappan; Fred W. Quantmeyer, Sr., Harrington Park; and Harold W. Tallman, Cresskill.

We are also indebted for the generous response of the following institutions; their librarians, curators, and editors: Allendale Historical Society; Aviation Hall of Fame of New Jersey; Bergen Community College Library; Bergen County Historical Society; Bergen County Police Department; Cliffside Park Public Library; Demarest Public Library; Edgewater Public Library; Elmwood Park Public Library; Englewood Public Library; New Jersey Room, Fairleigh Dickinson University, Rutherford; Fort Lee Public Library; Friends of the Hermitage; Garretson Forge and Farm; Glen Rock Public Library; Hasbrouck Heights Public Library; History of Wood-Ridge Committee; *Home and Store News*; Johnson Free Public Library; Meadowlands Museum; Midland Park Public Library; Midland Park Historical Society; Montvale Public Library; New Jersey Reference Division, Newark Public Library; New Jersey Bell; Library, New Jersey Department of Transportation; New Jersey Division of Archives and Records Management, Department of State; New Jersey Historical Society; New Milford Public Library; *The News*, Wykoff; North Arlington Historical Society; Northvale Public Library; Oakland Historical Society; Old Tappan Public Library; Oradell Public Library; Paramus Historical and Preservation Society; Pascack Historical Society; Passaic Public Library; Paterson Museum; Public Service Electric and Gas Company; *The Record*, Hackensack; *The Ridgewood NEWSpapers*; Ridgewood Public Library; River Vale Public Library; Department of Special Collections and Archives, Alexander Library, Rutgers University; Rutherford Public Library; Saddle River Historical Committee; and Upper Saddle River Historical Society.

We extend a special thanks to: Thomas J. Alrutz, Director, Newark Public Library; and his staff: Peter Silva, Robert Blackwell, and Syvella Copeland; Frederick Bunker, Rutherford Borough Historian; Virginia Mosley, Tenafly Borough Historian; Richard Kole; Jean-Rey Turner; Edward Skipworth, Alexander Library, Rutgers University; and Mary Damoorgian, New Jersey Room, Fairleigh Dickinson University, Rutherford.

Introduction

Bergen County is a distinctive place. From the dramatic cliffs of the Palisades to the rolling hills of the Hackensack valley, generation after generation have made comfortable lives for themselves there. As one drives through its suburban communities today, perhaps enjoying the pleasant tree-lined streets or, conversely, enduring the rush hour traffic, it is difficult to envision the panorama of woods and water courses which tempted European settlers over three hundred years ago, and which provided sustenance for paleolithic Indians some ten thousand years before. The rivers today flow almost unnoticed beneath the busy bridges which serve the needs of modern transportation. Little remains to remind the passerby of the water traffic which provided the impetus for early settlement and commercial growth. The mountains to the north and the meadows to the south offered both European and Indian access to abundant game. In between, where a rolling plain sloped toward the southeast, farmers could prosper on the fertile land.

Bergen County has now marked its three hundredth anniversary. Though diminished in size twice in its history by the formation of Passaic County in 1837 and Hudson County in 1840, the county today is the most populous in the state* and among the richest in industry and culture. This volume is meant to be a celebration of those people of Bergen through their three hundred years; the traders and settlers who knew the land and its original people long

*According to 1983 official State of New Jersey estimates

before the boundaries were drawn; the solid farmers who flourished there; the entrepreneurs with their factories and commerce; the immigrants who added new dimensions; and most recently the suburbanites and commuters whose "cottages" and "villas" sprouted around each new station on the rail line.

The commuters are still coming, of course, many of them unaware of important chapters in the history of their county. Bergenites concerned with pollution levels in their air and streams may be surprised to discover that just one hundred years ago rural Bergen County provided a place in the country for vacationing New Yorkers, with celebrated resort hotels catering to every whim. Thanks to the 1976 Bicentennial, many more may be familiar with the tensions which racked Bergen during the Revolution with Tory and patriot neighbors in constant conflict. Fewer, however, are likely to know of the suffering brought by the Civil War as Union supporters clashed with local "Copperheads" over support for the fighting, or the labor struggles of the 1920s and 1930s as industrial problems common across the nation hit home.

In addition to reflecting major themes in American history, Bergen made some significant contributions as well. This county played an important role in the history of American aviation with Anthony Fokker headquartered at Teterboro. In Radburn, the county boasts an internationally famous experiment in residential community design. The early history of the American motion picture industry was played out on the crest of the Palisades. The county that provided resort hotels and amusement parks to previous generations now draws crowds to its sports complex and its fabulous shopping centers.

A developer's dream both before and after the construction of the famous George Washington Bridge, Bergen's seventy municipalities have provided numerous opportunities for the increasing waves of city dwellers seeking homes of their own on what has been called "the crabgrass frontier." The evolving styles of these homes over the years are fascinating, as are the changing ways in which builders have tried to convince people to trade their fire escapes for lawn chairs. Bergen County today has been called "the ultimate suburb." Such terms evoke a series of predictable responses. Some such reactions are holdovers from the 1950s and 1960s when social critics pointed to what they saw as an insulated and sterile lifestyle in which competition for social status based on material wealth had replaced the more traditional and enduring values associated with earlier American communities. Suburbia in the 1980s is undergoing new changes. Some feel that the continuing insularity of the suburbs is undermining efforts to revitalize American cities. Others point out that the suburbs themselves are becoming urbanized in both their density of population and the increasingly complex patterns of living there.

Critics notwithstanding, however, thousands of families each week contact their real estate agents in hopes of buying in to what for most is still the American dream.

Researched with the cooperation of the Bergen County Historical Society and dozens of other libraries and local agencies, this book is intended to complement the more comprehensive pamphlet series designed for the tercentenary by the Bergen County Cultural and Heritage Commission. In a book such as this it would be impossible to do justice to every community or every important individual or event. Instead we seek here to evoke some of the feelings and experiences of ordinary people in their homes, at work, in their schools, entertaining themselves and one another, and to suggest how some of those patterns of aspiration and fulfillment have changed over time. A special effort has been made to describe the three-hundred-year history of Bergen in the context of the broader American experience.

The quality of the pictures published here is generally excellent, but we have made our choices primarily on the significance of the subject matter. In addition, emphasis has been placed on the period after 1860 for which the pictorial record is particularly strong. We will have succeeded if this book provides some measure of understanding about the people and events that have made Bergen County what it is today.

chapter 1

Bergen County historians generally agree that Lower Closter Dock below Alpine, later known as Huyler's Landing, was the site of the British invasion of Bergen County on November 20, 1776. This contemporary watercolor by Thomas Davies depicts the scene as observed by Lord Rawdon, an engineering officer who served under Cornwallis. Courtesy New York Public Library, Print Division

From Colony To State

When the General Assembly of East Jersey first legally defined the county of Bergen in 1683, the area had already been settled for fifty years, not a few of them tumultuous, as the Indians, the Dutch and the English contended for possession of the potential wealth of the new land.

The first Europeans to interest themselves in the area were represented by the Dutch West India Company which moved in the mid 1620s to exploit Henry Hudson's claim of 1609. Adventurers and traders, these early settlers were not really interested in transferring European culture to America. The earliest Dutch settlements in New Jersey, like those elsewhere in New Netherlands, were intended primarily to be trading outposts, not places for building home or raising families. In 1630 the first permanent settlement in New Jersey was planted at what was later called Paulus Hook, a point where several Indian trails came together across the Hudson from the tiny Dutch fortress at New Amsterdam. One of the founders of the Dutch West India Company, Michael Reynierse Paauw had taken advantage of his government's interest in encouraging people to come to its colony. He had been chartered as a patron, with the rights of a feudal baron over the estate which he named Pavonia (stretching over what is Hoboken and Jersey City today and until 1840 part of Bergen County) in return for his promise to transplant fifty settlers there. Although Paauw eventually failed to keep his pledge to deliver colonists, the site was so valuable that traders stayed on.

The earliest settlements in what is now Bergen County were destined to be short lived. Both David DeVries's outpost at Vriessendael (1640), which included the present borough of Edgewater; and Achter Col, a trading post on the east bank of the Hackensack River in modern Bogota, were destroyed by the Indians in 1643.

The Dutch authorities of New Netherlands tended to see the Indians as traders to be victimized rather than as neighbors to be lived with. Several of the Dutch governors, most nobably William Kieft who in 1643 ordered the massacre of scores of friendly natives, contributed to such troubles. Again in 1655 the Indians destroyed the settlements across the river from New Amsterdam and either killed the inhabitants or carried them off into captivity in a conflict which some believe might have been avoided with more enlightened leadership from the Dutch. Though not quite so heartless toward their fellow Europeans, governors like Kieft and Peter Stuyvesant were held in contempt by many of the colonists as well. Over time some of the people of New Netherlands had come to view the new world as more than a commercial investment, and had taken to constantly petitioning the mother country to grant them the rights of local self government and religious freedom.

By the late 1650s, when the colonists again turned their attention across the Hudson, more of them seemed ready to plant real roots. The village of Bergen (near today's Journal Square in Jersey City) was laid out in 1660 with thirty-two lots protected by a wooden palisade. In the middle was a common with a well to draw water for the colonists and their livestock, and a lot was set aside for construction of a church. Within a year Bergen had its own government with a sheriff (*schout* as the Dutch called him) and three local magistrates. The Dutch settlers of New Jersey had begun to think of the new world as home.

Under British rule the area began to show its full potential. Settlement moved deeper into the countryside. The British were more enlightened in dealing with the Indians and Oratam, the old and wise sachem of the Hackensack Indians who had found difficulty in dealing with the Dutch, lived to see permanent peace prevail. At the time the British assumed control over New Netherlands in 1664, Charles II had been restored to the throne after almost two decades of strife and civil war. Now, in gratitude for their support, King Charles and James the Duke of York granted the rights of proprietorship over the British colony of New Jersey to Lord Berkeley and Sir George Carteret who, in turn, sold or granted patents to large grants of land there. One of the earliest, a tract of 15,308 acres, went to William Sandford and Nathaniel Kingsland of Barbadoes. It lay between the Hackensack and Passaic Rivers south of today's East Rutherford. Another grant of 10,000 acres went to John Berry, also of Barbadoes. Berry's property, which also spanned the area between the two rivers, extended north to parts of Paramus and River Edge. For obvious reasons, the township came to be known as "New Barbadoes." The original tracts encompass more than twenty of the county's most prosperous communities today.

Quickly these and other patentees opened their lands, and within a decade men and women from the

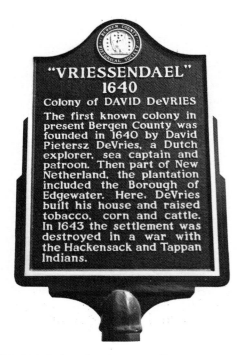

"VRIESSENDAEL"
1640
Colony of DAVID DeVRIES

The first known colony in present Bergen County was founded in 1640 by David Pietersz DeVries, a Dutch explorer, sea captain and patroon. Then part of New Netherland, the plantation included the Borough of Edgewater. Here, DeVries built his house and raised tobacco, corn and cattle. In 1643 the settlement was destroyed in a war with the Hackensack and Tappan Indians.

The historical marker commemorating Vriessendael was erected at Veterans Park, Edgewater by the Bergen County Historical Society. Courtesy Reginald McMahon

Oratam (Oratum, Oratamin, Oratamy, Oratani), sachem of the Hackensack Indians. Described by the historian William Nelson as a "notable man among notable men in his day," his name appears again and again in the treaties in which the Dutch attempted to resolve their difficulties with the Indians. This bronze bust is the work of sculptor John Ettle of Leonia who presented it to the Bergen County Historical Society in 1922. Courtesy Newark Public Library

other Dutch settlements at New Amsterdam, Brooklyn, Hoboken, and elsewhere moved west. One of the earliest of these inland settlements was at Old Bridge (now River Edge and New Milford) begun by French Huguenot David Demarest who established himself on the banks of the Hackensack in 1677. Like others of the patentees, in addition to his grant from the proprietors, Demarest also purchased his land from the Indians. This so called French Patent cost him as follows:

100 Fathem of Black Wampum	100 Barrs of Lead
100 Fathem of White Wampum	100 knives
15 Fire lock guns	one Barrell of Powder
15 Kettles	4 Barrels of Beer
20 Blanketts	One Saw
20 Match Coates I say Twenty	One Anker of Rum
20 hatchets	One Pistoll
20 hows	one Plaine
30 paire of Stockings	a Great Knife &
20 Shirts	one Carpenter Axe

(source: East Jersey Deeds and Commissions)

In the decades to come Bergen County was settled by a varied mixture of ethnic and national groups. French Huguenots came with David Demarest from New York. In addition to Barbadians, English also came from Long Island, settling in what came to be called the English Neighborhood (Ridgefield, Leonia, Englewood). Scots, Germans, Poles, and others too settled here. However, despite English rule and the varied mix of immigrants, Dutch culture and traditions continued to dominate life in Bergen in important ways for two hundred years or more. As the settlers moved across the river, they established Dutch Reformed churches. Habits of food and dress, methods of farming and housekeeping; all had this distinct Dutch flavor.

Historian Adrian Leiby in *The Early Dutch and Swedish Settlers of New Jersey* explained it as "a cheery self-confidence that the ways of the Dutch were better ways." The Dutch "industry, frugality, and assiduous perseverance" which Leiby describes must surely have impressed incoming settlers as did the "general air of hearty abundance that characterized Dutch farms throughout all of New York and New Jersey." It may be impossible to define in categorical terms why cultural patterns develop and persist as they do, but the prevalence of Dutch (or Dutch-influenced) language and culture gave to Bergen County a flavor of life different from any other corner of colonial America. To be sure, not everyone approved. Many outside observers thought that the simple ways of the "Jersey Dutch" as they were called, were boorish and unrefined in comparision with the more sophisticated lifestyles of New York or even the English-speaking countryside. But in ways, especially in its influence on place names and architecture, the Dutch inheritance has added a special charm to the history of Bergen County.

The Dutch stone farmhouse, for example, represents a unique type of colonial architecture which had no real prototype in Europe. The first permanent homes in the area were tiny cabins and cottages of wood or rough stone walls with board or thatched roofs. Windows were small because glass was rare, but also because settlers were still conscious of the danger of Indian attack. In overall appearance the design of these cottages must have recalled their builders' European heritage, but they already showed differences.

One distinctive characteristic which soon developed was a "double plan" which called for two roughly equal sized rooms, each with a separate entry from outside. The adjoining rooms were likely used by married sons or daughters and their families. In the eighteenth century as the area prospered, the homes tended to be built larger and with more attention to craftsmanship. More care was given, for example, to the finishing of the stone used for the facade. The stone used for such houses was frequently quarried not far from the site, and the labor of slaves was often important in performing the heavy work of moving and placing them. Two distinctive elements of roof design were developed as well. One was the curved overhanging eaves which extended several feet beyond the outside walls. Besides its charming appearance and sun-shading effect, the overhang served the very practical purpose of directing rain water away from the walls where it might have carried away the ordinary clay and straw used as mortar between the stones. Another distinctive roof innovation was the gambrel roof, which provided a large attic for working and storage space, and which became more and more typical as the eighteenth and nineteenth centuries progressed. Gambrel roofs in the Dutch style presented a more graceful profile than their boxy New England counterparts.

At the same time that new and larger homes were being built, the simpler ones of the preceding generations were being expanded. Sometimes a large main house was attached to the original cottage. The earlier structure was then used as slave quarters, or more typically, the kitchen wing. Another of the features of the Dutch style was the Dutch doors, split so that the top half could be opened independently. Some were decorated with "bulls eye" windows made of thick bottle glass. The dating of these old homes is sometimes made easier by the "date stones" which occasionally were built into the walls. Due to the expansion and renovation of homes over the years, however, they are not uniformly reliable.

After the Revolution and well into the nineteenth century, the Dutch style continued to predominate, but gradually the influence of English architectural styles became evident as they were incorporated with the older Dutch elements. It was a natural evolution, then, based upon the needs of the builders and the limits of the materials that were locally available that led to what architectural historian John Boyd has called the most

Captain John Berry, who owned extensive tracts of land in southern Bergen County in 1669. Other original patentees from Barbadoes included William Sandford and Nathaniel Kingsland. Courtesy Bergen County Historical Society

When the progenitor of the Banta family in America, Epke Jacobs, purchased 183 acres "lying and being upon the New Plantation upon the Hackensack River" in 1681, he was sixty-two years old and had already been in the new world for twenty years. He settled first on Long Island, after which he moved to Bergen County. Courtesy New York Public Library; United States History, Local History & Genealogy Division

Led by the mark of Assowakon, sachem of Tappan, Indian pictographs decorate the English translation of a Dutch deed for a tract of land near Haverstraw, New York, purchased by Balthazer de Hart in 1671. The deed identifies the property as being part of the "Province of New Jersey." Boundary lines between the two states were disputed for one hundred years until a line was finally agreed upon in 1769. Courtesy Archives Section, New Jersey Division of Archives and Records Management

individual and distinctive domestic architecture of colonial America. During the eighteenth century these dwellings achieved a harmony of design and function which is the source of their lasting appeal even now when most of them can no longer be appreciated in their original settings of lush meadows and rolling hills.

Another important element of the Dutch-influenced culture which remained long after the British had come to rule was the Dutch Reformed church. Just as the first churches in New England were Congregational and in Virginia Anglican; in Bergen County they were Dutch Reformed. Long after "Jersey Dutch" began to be supplanted by English in everyday speech, the Reformed churches predominated. As late as 1850 there were more than a few towns in which the Dutch-speaking church was the only church, and many a sermon must have served more to frustrate than to sanctify the spirits of the growing number of worshipers who could not understand the language.

We know less about the architectural history of the churches. The earliest of them, like the church built at Bergen (Jersey City) in the early 1660s, were either rectangular, hexagonal, or octagonal in design. Inside there would be benches along the walls for the men. Women and children would sit in the center under the hanging bell rope on chairs they had brought from home. There are no remaining examples of the earliest Dutch colonial churches, in large part because eighteenth and nineteenth century congregations tended to build their new churches with the stones from the older ones. The churches that do remain date from the 1790s and the early 1800s when the influence of English architectural designs had already taken hold.

The Dutch Reformed churches in New York and New Jersey, like Calvinist congregations across New England and the rest of the colonies, were racked by religious controversy during the eighteenth century. The Great Awakening, as it was called, pitched younger ministers, some of whom were trained in America and preferred a more animated and emotional religious experience, against the older and predominantly European trained clergy who practiced more traditional forms of worship and maintained a close association with the European hierarchy. These were colonists who took their religion seriously. Formerly close-knit congregations, friends and even families were split by such passionate disagreements. By 1756 the line had been clearly drawn between the "new light" or *coetus* and the "old light" or *conferentie* ministers who had organized to combat the former. Because of its influential young minister, John Henry Goetschius, the Bergen County area of Schraalenburgh had become in the words of one historian "the capital of the Great Awakening in the Dutch Reformed church." His influence was evident among the next generation of Dutch Reformed parsons in America. There were exceptions, but the tendency when the American Revolution came was for the followers of *coetus* preachers to support the American cause and the *conferentie* to side with the British authorities.

These religious overtones explain some of the experience of the Revolution in Bergen County, but geography was at least as important a factor. In July 1776, General Washington chose the Palisades for the construction of what was to be called Fort Lee, directly across the

The above receipt signed by Casparus Zabreski in 1743-44, illustrates the pervasiveness of the Dutch language in Bergen County. Although of Polish descent, Zabreski, one of the numerous descendants of Albrecht Zaberowskij, an early Bergen County settler, found it convenient to do business in Jersey Dutch. The translation reads: "I receive from Peeteres Debaan the sum of 18 shillings and 4 pennies for cream and cream and this and that. I admit that he paid the full amount and satisfied the full amount, and all bills between he and I are paid in full. By me, Casp. Zabreski." Courtesy Bergen County Historical Society

Hudson from Fort Washington, a second new fortress on Manhattan. Artillery from both forts and from a temporary battery below the bluff harassed British ships on the Hudson. After Fort Washington fell into British hands in 1776, General Cornwallis lost no time in invading New Jersey to neutralize the fortifications at Fort Lee. Washington's timely retreat from the larger English forces allowed him to turn the tide just weeks later at Trenton and Princeton.

The story of Bergen County's role in the War for American Independence has been fully chronicled by Adrian Leiby in *The Revolutionary War in the Hackensack Valley: The Jersey Dutch and the Neutral Ground, 1777-1783*. Although there were no great battles fought here, the patriotic citizens of Bergen may have been tested more than those anywhere else in the colonies. In the "neutral ground," as it was called, between the British in New York and the Continental Army to the west, neither force held permanent control. With tacit approval from General Clinton in New York, Tory raiding parties swept down upon settlements which supported the Americans. The patriots, of course, responded in kind and the resulting situation brought destruction to much of the countryside. Leiby quotes one artillery officer's report that the "formerly delightful village of Schraalenburgh" had been "reduced to a heap of rubbish" by such a raid. Although most of those who suffered through the Revolution in Bergen County were victims of scattered and isolated incidents, there were several significant engagements. In River Vale in September 1778, a body of light dragoons under Col. George Baylor was pounced upon by the British in the middle of the night and massacred. In March of 1780 the British attacked and burned Hackensack. There were also patriot raids including one abortive attack on a Tory-held block house at Bulls Ferry.

Although they could not maintain control of Bergen County, the area was so strategically important that continental troops were often in the area. Today scores of stories remain about local landmarks which served as barracks for militiamen or headquarters for Revolutionary officers. In few other parts of America can it be said of so many sites that "George Washington slept here."

It is difficult to document that Washington actually used the Ackerman-Zabriskie-Steuben House, but this

This decorated manuscript found in a Hopper family Bible records one family's shift from the Dutch language to the use of English in recording their vital statistics. Courtesy Mrs. Earl Baer, Upper Saddle River

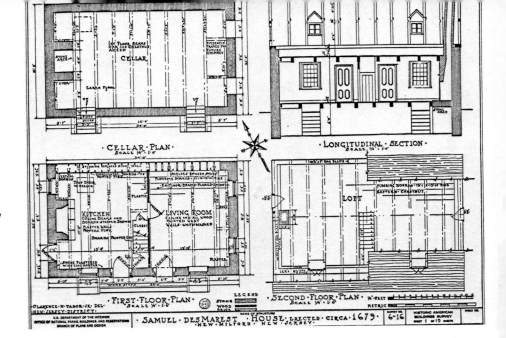

The Samuel Demarest house from New Milford built in the early 1700s, has the double entry and the overhanging eaves common to later colonial homes. The floor plan drawn by the Historic American Buildings Survey shows that the house was really one room deep, with the kitchen serving as a "family room." The adjoining room, with its separate entry, very likely was used by the family of a son or daughter. In some such "double plan" houses there were kitchens for each side. The house is shown here in 1957 after it had been moved and reconstructed on the grounds of the Bergen County Historical Society in River Edge. Courtesy Newark Public Library

site deserves special mention because its history represents each phase of Bergen County's colonial and revolutionary past. Originally developed by David Ackerman, a seventeenth century Bergen County pioneer, the farm and attendant tidal mill were purchased in 1745 by Jan Zabriskie whose fortunes prospered from traffic on the river. In 1777, the property was confiscated by the State of New Jersey because Jan's son John had fled to New York to the protection of the King. Washington's troops had passed the house the year before on their retreat from Fort Lee, to be followed only days later by triumphant British columns. The abandoned house was also used during a number of British raids on the Hackensack valley between 1777 and 1780. At alternate times during the same period it accommodated patriot officers as well, and it is believed by some to have served as Washington's headquarters in September of 1780. After the war a grateful New Jersey presented the property to Baron Von Steuben for his contributions to American freedom. But the Baron never spent any time on the Hackensack. Instead he sold the property 5 years later to an aide who, in turn, sold it to John Zabriskie, grandson of the loyalist from whom it had been confiscated. In 1928 it was acquired by the State, and subsequently restored as a historic site. Since 1939 it has served as the headquarters and museum of the Bergen County Historical Society. Today the Steuben House, like dozens of other historical landmarks across the county, serves to remind us of the contributions made by the sturdy patriots of Bergen to an emerging American nation.

The Jack Terhune homestead, built in Wyckoff in the early 1700s, is typical of primitive Bergen County stone houses. It was built of rough stone with narrow windows and at first probably had a thatched roof. Courtesy Bergen County Historical Society

The Haring-De Wolf house stands near the golf course on De Wolf Road in Old Tappan. Although wider and deeper after expansion than the Demarest house, the floor plan is similar. The gambrel roof, which became another distinguishing feature of the Dutch style, provided a roomy garret for storage and work space. The frame wing by the well sweep was a later addition and is now considerably altered. Heavy posts and a roof have been added to create a porch since this picture was taken in the 1920s. Courtesy Special Collections, Alexander Library, Rutgers University

The Roelof Westervelt House, 81 Westervelt Avenue, Tenafly, was expanded year after year. The small stone section was a kitchen addition to the main section built circa 1798-1800, and the frame wing was added in 1825. The spacious attic resounded again to the clack of looms when the Tenafly Weavers operated a crafts shop and tearoom on the premises in the early 1930s. Courtesy New Jersey Room, Fairleigh Dickinson University, Rutherford

Begun as a tiny farmhouse in the first quarter of the eighteenth century, the Ackerman-Brinkerhoff house was later expanded with a large gambrel-roofed addition. The house stood on Polifly Road in Hasbrouck Heights until 1974 when it was demolished to make room for a high-rise office building. Area residents remember its final years as the Stagg Farm, a seasonal produce market. Courtesy Special Collections, Alexander Library, Rutgers University

Recent investigations during the Bergen County Early Stone House Survey indicate that the kitchen wing of the Jacobus Demarest House was a subsequent addition to the original structure. Located at 618 River Road in River Edge, the house still retains its Dutch doors, one at each end of a spacious center hall. A date stone to the left of the front entrance reads "1765." Courtesy Newark Public Library

As the "Dutch Colonial" style evolved, the main section and the wing were sometimes built at the same time, as in the Ferdon House on 14th Street in Norwood. This photograph was taken circa 1912 before the addition of attic dormers and veranda to the larger section of the house. Courtesy Claire K. Tholl

The front and rear verandas, and the carved interior moldings of the Vreeland House in Leonia (once part of the English Neighborhood) reflect the Georgian-Federal designs which reached their height in Bergen County local architectural traditions in the first half of the nineteenth century. Located at 125 Lake Avenue, the house is briefly visible to traffic on Route 80. Photo from Wendenhack, Early Dutch Houses of New Jersey

The octagonal church at Bergen (Jersey City) as imagined by an artist many years later. Courtesy Newark Public Library

By the turn of the nineteenth century, the Hackensack Valley had five new churches of native sandstone. The simplicity and dignity of these churches, as well as the ones of similar style, are as important architecturally as are Bergen's Dutch farmhouses. The First Reformed Church of Hackensack, the prototype in Bergen County, built in 1791 and later enlarged, contains the irregular stones from the two buildings which preceded it. A close-up of one wall reveals the initials of earlier church members below the stone tablet originally placed over the door and moved during alterations in the 1840s. The barely visible motto—Een-draght maakt Macht, "Union is Strength"—appears above the crowned lion representing William of Orange. The tablet was damaged by a lightning bolt in 1795, alarming some members who saw it as a sign of divine displeasure at divisions in the congregation. Courtesy Newark Public Library

The Church of the Ponds, stood in what is now Oakland. It was constructed in a simple style reflecting that of its larger sisters to the southeast. Although early records have been lost, tradition traces this Dutch Reformed congregation to a log church erected circa 1710 in Franklin Lakes. The old building has not survived, but a replica built with some salvaged parts serves as the Oakland Public Library. Courtesy Historical American Buildings Survey, Library of Congress

Located as it was near a number of roads of historic importance, the Dutch Reformed Church at Paramus played many roles during the Revolution both as a continental army outpost, and hospital, and as a target for British raids. A new church was built alongside the old in 1800 and now presides in quiet dignity over Route 17 in Ridgewood. *Courtesy Special Collections, Alexander Library, Rutgers University*

The South Schraalenburgh Church in Bergenfield was built in 1799 after the Dutch Reformed congregation had divided over doctrinal issues. In 1822, with other disaffected members of the Dutch church at Hackensack, the congregation seceded from the Dutch Reformed Church to form the True Dutch Reformed Church in South Hackensack. Led by Rev. Solomon Froeligh, the new church was active in Bergen County until the end of the nineteenth century, at which time it merged with the Presbyterian and Christian Reformed churches. The congregation is now known as the South Presbyterian Church. *Courtesy Special Collections, Alexander Library, Rutgers University*

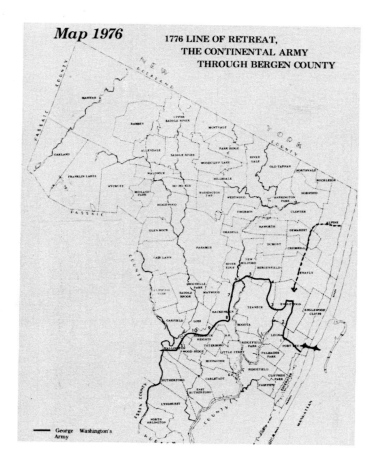

Map 1976

**1776 LINE OF RETREAT,
THE CONTINENTAL ARMY
THROUGH BERGEN COUNTY**

George Washington's Army

This map of modern Bergen County shows the route of Washington's retreat in November 1776. Two hundred years later, Bergen County citizens re-enacted the famous march during their American Revolution Bicentennial celebration. According to historical research previously noted, the dotted line indicating the British advance should begin farther south on the Hudson, opposite Cresskill. Courtesy of Bergen County '76 Retreat Committee

When George Washington made this house his headquarters during the critical week before his retreat from Fort Lee in 1776, it was the home of the patriot Peter Zabriskie, who built it by the Green circa 1751. The original structure was later enlarged and remodeled as "The Mansion House," a tavern and hotel, and survived until October 1945 when it was demolished for "commercial improvement." Courtesy Bergen County Historical Society

The Ackerman-Zabriskie-Steuben House on the Hackensack River at New Bridge as sketched by Claire K. Tholl. Other architectural details shown here were drawn for the Historic American Buildings Survey in 1935. Now the headquarters of the Bergen County Historical Society, the house is open for visitors on a regular schedule. Courtesy Bergen County Historical Society

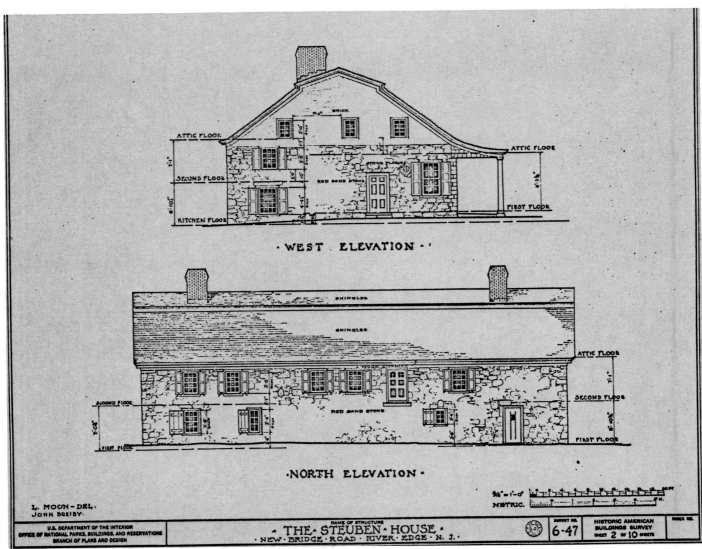

In November 1782, Johannis Haring of Harrington Township inventoried the losses he had personally sustained from the enemy. They included three horses, nine milk cows, two cattle, nineteen sheep, one gun, and one Negro about 17 years old. *Courtesy Archives Section, New Jersey Division of Archives and Records Management*

When Washington's letters were headed "Ramapough," he is believed to have stayed in what is now Mahwah at Andrew Hopper's house on Ramapo Valley Road, an important military route during the Revolution. The house has since been completely rebuilt, but the fireplace, or mantel, at which the general allegedly warmed himself has been preserved. *From Lossing,* Pictorial Field Book of the Revolution, *1859*

When Washington came to Hackensack in 1780 to attend Enoch Poor's funeral, he undoubtedly visited the Westervelt-Lozier house where the general from New Hampshire lay in state. General Poor was interred with great ceremony in the cemetery of the old Church on the Green. The house, which stood at Main and Ward Streets, was razed in 1946. Poor's statue (inset) still faces the Bergen County courthouse. Courtesy New Jersey Historical Society; inset courtesy Newark Public Library

If George Washington were to return to the Hermitage on Franklin Turnpike in Ho-Ho-Kus, he would no doubt find it difficult to recognize the old stone farmhouse beneath its Gothic Revival embellishments. His hostess there was Theodosia Prevost, whose wealth and charm had won for her the friendship of a number of distinguished patriots, among them Aaron Burr, whom she married after the death of her British officer husband. After many years of neglect, the house was placed on the National Register in 1970 and is the first site in Bergen County to become a National Historic Landmark. Photo by John Kosta. Courtesy Friends of the Hermitage

On his way from Pompton to Suffern, New York, Washington spent the night of July 14, 1777 in the Van Allen house on Ramapo Valley Road in Oakland. Since this 1967 picture, the dormers and porch roof of the main section have been removed in the restoration undertaken by the town and the Oakland Historical Society whose headquarters it has become. *Courtesy Newark Public Library*

Tradition places Washington's Englewood headquarters at the house shown here, which later became the Liberty Pole Tavern. A small shopping center now occupies the site on the northeast corner of Palisades Avenue and Tenafly Road. *Courtesy Englewood Public Library*

chapter 2

When this picture was taken, water still turned the wheel of the old grist mill in Ramsey. Located on a stream which flowed southwest from Garrison's ice pond, this was one of the two mills on the former Christie tract, twenty-five acres located between Franklin Turnpike and what is now Lake Street. *Courtesy Home and Store News, Ramsey*

Living Off The Land

After the excitement of the Revolution, Bergen settled back into the solitude of its earlier pastoral existence. Between 1800 and the outbreak of the Civil War transportation routes were pressed through the region and prospering mills began the transformation to larger factories. Bergen County was still basically farming country, however, and it would remain so through most of the nineteenth century.

Farming, of course, had been the main activity of Bergen settlers from the beginning as they earned their living from the soil. It did not take long, however, for farmers to take advantage of commercial opportunities. Bergen County grain was traded to the West Indies early in the colonial period, and early on the pattern was set for Bergen farmers concentrating much of their effort in growing fruits and vegetables for consumers in New York and in manufacturing areas in northern New Jersey.

The layout of a typical Bergen County farm before the Civil War revealed immediately the richness and productivity of the soil. The comfortable, but not over-large, farmhouse was typically surrounded with a cluster of outbuildings for the processing and storage of products and for the housing of livestock. The Jacob Zabriskie farm in Paramus provides an interesting example. Although only a few of the original structures remain standing today, the historians of the Historic American Buildings Survey have documented for us what the place once looked like. Common sights were barns constructed in the Dutch style with high pitched roofs and low side walls, and the distinctive Dutch hay barrack with its four poles stuck in the ground covered by a roof which could be raised or lowered. It is not difficult to imagine the spacious farmhouse attics, the barns and smokehouses packed with the bounty of the land. Local newspapers of the time were known to boast regularly about the quality of Bergen crops: pears that weighed up to a pound, celery three feet long, and potatoes ten inches long and nine inches around.

From the earliest days Bergen farmers made good use of the meadows, harvesting the salt hay for cattle fodder and developing sweet meadows for grain and pasturage. As late as the 1890s salt hay was used around Little Ferry in ice houses and for bedding the horses in area stables. Various attempts at developing other cash crops met with little success. Efforts at tobacco growing and flax culture were short lived. But there was one product of

nineteenth century Bergen farms which won national fame—the strawberry. Cultivated for the New York market as early as 1800, by 1850 strawberry farming had developed into a thriving business. New and improved varieties were developed and the boom spread to Ramsey and Allendale where, beginning in the 1850s, freight trains on the new Erie Railroad line were loaded nightly in June and July with local berries for the New York market. By 1859 the strawberry crop approached ten to fifteen million baskets annually. However, competition with other states and focus on vegetable growing had all but eliminated Bergen's strawberry business by the end of the century.

As industrial activity and population grew in cities such as Paterson, Newark and New York, so did demand for Bergen County's agricultural products. What had begun as subsistence farming developed into sophisticated commercial enterprise. Organizations such as the New York Society for the Promotion of Agricultural Arts and Manufacturing and later the Bergen County Agricultural Society provided forums for the interchange of information on crop rotation, field drainage, improved plowing methods, and the use of lime, manure and commercial fertilizers. Farmers also became more politically involved as they began to agitate for improved roads and bridges to facilitate the trip to market.

Although agriculture was certainly the primary activity, over the centuries Bergen County's natural resources provided the raw materials for a variety of other commercial enterprises. Iron and copper were mined during the colonial period with significant results. The Bergen County iron industry flourished in the area which is now Passaic County, but the Schuyler Copper Mine remained Bergen's own. We find mention of the mine as early as 1715, and for the next two centuries the production of copper flourished or faltered as a variety of companies coped with the problem of flooding in the low-lying shafts. Lumbering was also a colonial occupation, but by the nineteenth century Bergen's forests had been depleted to the extent that the Anderson brothers of Hackensack found it necessary to import timber from Virginia for their lumber yard. Abundant clay along the Hackensack River from New Bridge to Moonachie gave rise to brick manufacture and pottery works in the nineteenth century.

Bergen County's many water courses accommodated

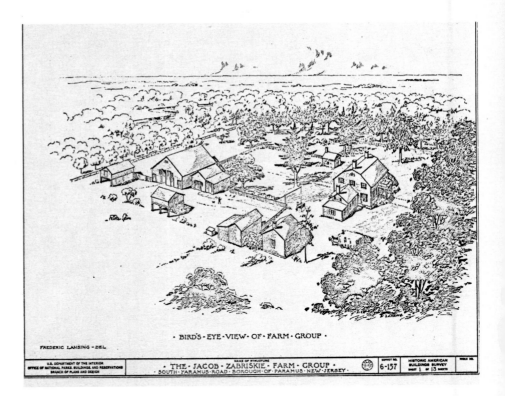

The Jacob Zabriskie farm on Paramus Road, as sketched by the Historic American Buildings Survey in 1935, included barns, workshop, sleigh house, shed, and grain and corn cribs. Today only the well and stone out-kitchen remain. The inset shows details of the sandstone smoke house where ham, bacon, pork and fish were preserved. Courtesy Historic American Buildings Survey, Library of Congress

the grist and saw mills necessary to support an agrarian culture. Colonial entrepreneurs dammed the brooks and streams which fed the Saddle River, the Hackensack, the Ramapo; and on Bergen's southern boundary, the Passaic, using water power for increasingly sophisticated manufactures such as textile mills, iron foundries, and in the 1850s, furniture factories.

Among other business enterprises, Kirkbride's *New Jersey Business Directory* of 1850 lists forty-seven feed and saw mills, eleven textile mills, two foundries and four distilleries. The industry unique to Bergen County, however, was located in what is now Park Ridge, where the Campbell family had been manufacturing wampum since the last quarter of the 1700s.

Among the entrepreneurs of Bergen County, John Campbell and his sons are remembered for their local industry which played a part in the "conquering" of the American West. In 1775 Campbell had set up to manufacture in volume the strings of drilled and polished shells with which the colonists had learned to trade with the Indians. The business grew from a cottage industry in Campbell's home to a full-fledged factory which supplied, among other Western traders, the famous John Jacob Astor. The Campbells collected their conch and clam shells from New York City fish markets, returning on the Hackensack River with ten or twelve barrels at a time. Part of each load was sold to farmers' wives and daughters who were skilled in the craft. The finished strings would be re-sold to the Campbells or to storekeepers in the area who acted as their representatives. It was reported in 1844 that a woman could produce between five and ten strings per day for which she received 12½ cents per string.

Sometime before 1850 two of the Campbell sons invented a drilling machine which increased dramatically the production of wampum "pipes," the cylindrical ornaments the Indians wore on their garments or in their hair. The workings of the machine were a closely guarded secret. It was operated in the locked second floor room of the Campbell's factory, or "mint," on Pascack Creek. As the Indians in the West were gradually dispossessed—trading their rich lands for trinkets produced in the Bergen woods—the Campbell's business gradually died out.

The Campbells made good use of the oldest network of transportation in the area, the river system. The Hackensack, which was navigable as far north as New Milford, had carried lumber, iron, applejack and farm products to market since the late 1600s. As commerce and industry increased, so did the river traffic, with sloops, schooners and piraguas, (windjammers, as steamboat captains would later call them) coursing up and down the river. River traffic diminished with the coming of the railroads. Although a few schooners were still in use as late as in the early 1900s, inevitably the more prosaic steamboats had taken over the trade.

The Hudson River was also of special importance to Bergen County. Fort Lee dock (known as Burdett's Ferry) had been a river port from colonial times. A short distance above the landing, a break in the Palisades allowed egress to the valleys sheltered by this formidable barrier. Until the advent of the railroads, farm produce from the northern part of the county also found its way to the New York markets via Huyler's Landing Road, north of Fort Lee on the river.

The demands of commerce and trade also stimulated

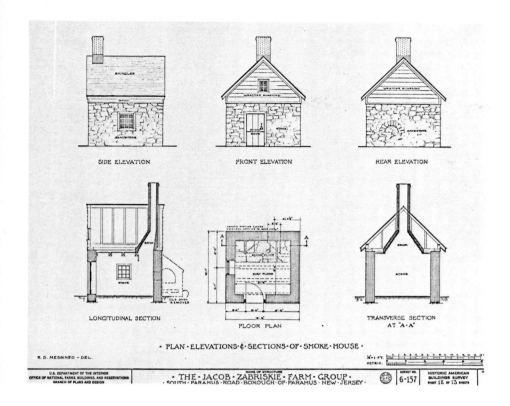

SIDE ELEVATION   FRONT ELEVATION   REAR ELEVATION

LONGITUDINAL SECTION   FLOOR PLAN   TRANSVERSE SECTION AT "A-A"

· PLAN · ELEVATIONS · & · SECTIONS · OF · SMOKE · HOUSE ·

R. D. MESSINEO - DEL.

U.S. DEPARTMENT OF THE INTERIOR
OFFICE OF NATIONAL PARKS, BUILDINGS, AND RESERVATIONS
BRANCH OF PLANS AND DESIGN

· THE · JACOB · ZABRISKIE · FARM · GROUP ·
· SOUTH · PARAMUS · ROAD · BOROUGH · OF · PARAMUS · NEW · JERSEY ·

SURVEY NO. 6-157

HISTORIC AMERICAN BUILDINGS SURVEY
SHEET 12 of 15 SHEETS

"internal improvements" undertaken by turnpike companies whose profits depended upon tolls collected at the pike or pole which was turned to allow the traveler to proceed. The Bergen Turnpike Company, incorporated in 1802, was the first in the county, and the third to be chartered in the state of New Jersey. Opened in 1804, the toll road's right-of-way had been in private hands for over one hundred years before Public Service transferred its control to the Bergen County Board of Chosen Freeholders in 1915.

In the 1840s and 1850s wooden planks laid along some roads protected the wagon wheels from the sometimes marshy passage, and provided a smoother ride. The cost of maintaining the planking became prohibitive, however, and one by one the plank roads were abandoned. Although macadam has long since paved the Paterson Plank Road in southern Bergen County, it is still referred to by its former name.

Without question the railroads provided the major catalyst which was to transform Bergen County from a peaceful agrarian region into a collection of bustling suburbs. As early as 1832, the Paterson and Hudson River Railroad had connected Paterson and Acquackanonk (now Passaic). Two years later the route was completed across southern Bergen County to Jersey City. Horses pulled the first trains, but soon the sound of steam engines was echoing across the fields. Traffic picked up in the 1850s as connections were completed through New Jersey between the terminus of the Erie line at Piermont, New York and the Hudson River ferries. May 26, 1859, marked the gala opening of the Northern Railroad of New Jersey, when the offical train rolled south from Piermont carrying officals and invited guests through the Bergen County towns of Norwood, Closter, Demarest, Cresskill, Tenafly, Englewood and Leonia to Jersey City, the southern terminus. The original schedule provided for a single passenger train per day each way. The most significant growth of the railroads, however, and their most obvious impact on the Bergen County lifestyle was to come after the Civil War.

The rivers, the turnpikes and the railroads provided increasing access to expanding markets and labor supply, encouraging the growth of Bergen County industry. Textile manufacture was the county's most important industry, with ten or more establishments in 1850 producing cotton and woolen yarns, cotton batting, candle wicking and "hair cloth," or horsehair fabrics (primarily for upholstery). These in turn spawned peripheral businesses for dyeing and processing fabrics such as Robert Rennie's Calico Print Works at Lodi, or the Boiling Spring Bleachery in what is now East Rutherford. Bergen industries were undoubtedly slowed by nationwide financial crises in 1837 and again in 1857, but even in the latter year we can find new industries being established such as John Dater's carriage factory in Ramsey and the Colignon Brothers chair factory in Old Tappan.

Most of the amenities of life in Bergen County before the Civil War had to do with the fresh air and lush countryside, but there were other amusements as well. Among them were noisy Fourth of July celebrations in Hackensack and elsewhere. At one such festival in 1824, General Lafayette returned to pay his respects at the grave of Revolutionary War hero Enoch Poor. Every now and then the Campbell brothers would set out a few bushels of

A typical Dutch barn with high pitched roof and low side walls dominated the out buildings of the William De Clark farm on Piermont Road in Closter when this picture was taken in 1937. Stalls for the farm animals stood along the low side walls and the high loft was used for grain and fodder. The double doors front and back were large enough to accommodate a horse and wagon. Photo by R. M. Lacey, Historic Buildings Survey, Library of Congress

The Dutch hay barrack persisted in Bergen County into the twentieth century. In this photograph taken on a farm in the Hackensack area circa 1889, the holes used for raising and lowering the roof are clearly visible. Courtesy Paramus Historical and Preservation Society

clams and oysters for the local folk to enjoy—as long as they were careful not to break the shells. Boating was popular with the well-to-do. For the more intellectually minded residents of Fort Lee there was a local debating society set up in 1838. For its first debate the group chose the perennial topic: "Slanderer or Seducer: Which is the Greatest Evil in Society?" In addition to their use as tax and polling centers, local hotels provided other social diversions.

Much of the conversation wherever Bergenites gathered in the late 1850s must have centered about the issues dividing North and South. Some of these same issues, as it turned out, divided Bergen. As one of the richer counties in the state, Bergen was also one of the largest slaveholding areas. Even after the state legislature passed the law providing for the gradual abolition of slavery in New Jersey in 1804, the institution faded very gradually there. In the census of 1830 there were still hundreds of slaves in Bergen County. Although that number had been reduced to 41 by 1850, there was still considerable pro-slavery sentiment.

In 1860 New Jersey became the only Northern state to cast electoral votes against Abraham Lincoln. Partly because of the textile manufactures who feared disruption of their Southern suppliers, and partly because of the close proximity to Democratic dominated New York City, Bergen harbored a vigorous opposition to the Republican Lincoln. Throughout the Civil War, despite the county's generous contributions of men and money to the cause of the Union, local politicans led by state Senator Daniel Holsman supported the vain efforts of the "Copperheads" (anti-war Democrats) on both the state and federal levels. Little had changed politically by 1865. Although in 1870 Republicans won over New Jersey's legislature and the state's votes went to Ulysses S. Grant in 1872, Democrats would continue to dominate Bergen's politics until almost the turn-of-the-century.

The Garretson Forge and Farm on River Road in Fair Lawn as it appeared before extensive alterations in 1902 added the present gambrel roof and pillared porch. Although the exact location of the forge has yet to be determined, boxes of iron work such as Dutch-style hinges, hooks and nails have been found in the cellar of the house, giving rise to the supposition that the forge may have also supplied the needs of neighboring farms. The house, built by Peter Garretson shortly after 1719, is now being restored by the Garretson Forge and Farm Restoration. Photo from the collection of Alieda Van De Giesen, courtesy of The Ridgewood NEWSpapers

The salt hay harvest in "Jersey Meadows," an oil painted circa 1865-1875 by Martin Johnson Heade (1819-1904), Pennsylvania aritst noted for his representation of marshlands. Courtesy Smith College Museum of Art

Families of many Bergen County strawberry farmers spent winter evenings weaving baskets of hickory splints gathered in the woods. Each grower added a distinctive mark in an attempt to insure his own baskets' safe return from the market. Pickers often covered the baskets of berries with oak leaves to preserve the freshness of the fruit. Courtesy Bergen County Historical Society

Berry pickers from cities and surrounding villages included school children dismissed early to help with the harvest which usually ran from the first of June through the middle of July. Farmers paid the laborers one cent per basket on which they would realize from two to five cents profit. From Industries of New Jersey, Part 6, Hudson, Passaic and Bergen Counties

Organized by local farmers in 1849, the Bergen County Farmers' Mutual Fire Insurance Company practiced conservative management of the firm's capital. As the reprinted 1853 advertisement suggests, they were also aware of the threat posed by careless smokers. Note the traditional Bergen County names listed among the directors. The company lasted until the end of the century when a series of fires combined with decreasing farm acreage led to its demise. Courtesy Bergen County Historical Society

BERGEN COUNTY
Farmers' Mutual Fire Insurance Company.
CHARTERED IN 1849.

THIS Company was organized for the benefit of the farmers of this and the neighboring Counties, and its operations continue to be limited to the original design. The By-Laws absolutely prohibit the insurance of all property usually denominated hazardous; also any property within a limited distance from buildings on adjoining premises. The rates of Premium are prepared for and adapted to none but the safest classes of risks. Every Policy is accompanied with an entire copy of the By Laws, which contain full and plain directions and conditions, enabling every member to ascertain what is requisite in any case to protect his insurance.

The first policy of this Company bears date May 1, 1849. The whole number of Policies issued up to January 1, 1853, was 715. The Premium notes received amounted to $9552.26, and the cash Premiums paid in, $286.02, and $190.16 had been received for interest arising from the cash capital. The whole amount of losses by fire, and all the incidental expenses of the Company, since its formation, was $771.54, leaving cash in hand to the amount of $2286.64.

No assessment on the Premium Notes has ever been made. Applications for insurance and surveys of property are subjected to the scrutiny of a competent Committee of Directors, before approval. Agents are under bond, with sureties, to comply with the instructions of the Company.

Directors.

GARRET S. DEMAREST,	HENRY N. VOORHIS,	JOHN J. VAN BUSKIRK,	HENRY H. VOORHIS,
JOHN ACKERMAN,	CHARLES HASBROUCK,	ISAAC D. DEMAREST,	NICHOLAS C. DURIE,
JOHN J. DEMAREST,	GEORGE T. BRICKELL,	CORNELIUS C. ZABRISKIE,	JACOB J. FERDON,
	WILLIAM BLAIR.		

HENRY H. VOORHIS, *Secretary.*   **GARRET S. DEMAREST,** *President.*
ISAAC D. DEMAREST, *Treasurer.*   **JOHN ACKERMAN,** *Vice President.*

SPRING VALLEY, N. J., January 1st, 1853. ———

☞ Persons insured are particularly cautioned against smoking pipes, or cigars, in or near their barns, &c.

DAILY ADVERTISER PRINT—OFFICE CORNER OF BROAD AND BANK STREET, NEWARK N.J.

The Zabriskie Mill on the Saddle River in what is now Paramus, was in operation before 1745 as a grist mill, a saw mill, and in the nineteenth century, a textile mill. Its color gave rise to the name of its locality, Red Mill. The inset shows the Easton Tower which was built on the site after the original mill was torn down in 1894. The tower's wheel provided water for the fountains and ponds on the estate of Edward D. Easton, founder of the Columbia Gramaphone Company. Once one of the most photographed of Bergen County landmarks, the tower was restored in 1967 by the Bergen County Park Commission. Its once-spacious setting has been carved up by intersecting highways, the Paramus and Saddle River Roads, and Route 4. Courtesy Ridegwood Public Library; inset courtesy Paterson Museum

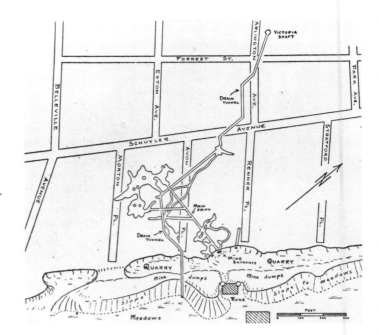

The shafts and tunnels of the Schuyler Copper Mine are shown here superimposed upon a modern street grid of North Arlington. The first steam engine in North America was installed here by Josiah Hornblower in 1755 to pump water from the mine. Map from Woodward, Copper Mines and Mining in New Jersey. *Courtesy Newark Public Library*

The little building which housed the Campbell wampum factory in Park Ridge gave no hint of the role that it played in the "conquering" of the American continent as western traders tempted the Indians with wampum and shell jewelry polished and drilled on the Campbell's machine. *Courtesy Bergen County Historical Society*

An invention of James and David Campbell, the machine pictured was able to drill six "pipes" at the same time in a process known only to the Campbell family. *Courtesy Bergen County Historical Society*

In the 1830s, the Anderson brothers' schooner was a familiar sight on the Hackensack River as it plied between their lumber yard in Hackensack and their 3000 acre Virginia plantation, which provided their timber. In addition to their New York City trade, the yard provided fuel for steamboats before the latter swtiched to coal. After John C. Z. Anderson's death in 1836 his brother David I. moved to what is now Wallington and engaged in a new venture destined to become another Anderson's Lumber Yard. Situated on either side of the Passaic River at the foot of Gregory Avenue in Passaic, the firm continued until well into the twentieth century. *Courtesy Bergen County Historical Society*

The home in Wallington, built by David I. Anderson on property formerly owned by Walling Van Winkle, one of the original settlers of Wallington, and one of the eight Wallings for whom the town was named. Anderson's home between the Passaic River and Zabriskie Avenue was convenient to his lumber yard on the river. *Courtesy Grace Speer Photograph Collection, Passaic Public Library*

In this picture, taken after the Civil War, employees pose before the Wortendyke Mills in what is now Midland Park. Three generations of Wortendykes had been engaged in textile manufacture here since the first Cornelius established his wool-carding mill in 1812. His son Abraham changed the product from wool to cotton. At the time of his death in 1857, the mills were producing batting and candle wicking for which the grandson, Cornelius A., obtained a number of patents. In 1874, in the midst of a financial panic, the latter expanded into the production of silk, establishing the first silk mill in Bergen County. Courtesy Midland Park Historical Society

Bogert's mill in Harrington Park, pictured here after it had been rebuilt in 1867, was operated by the Bogert family for more than 150 years. The property was sold to the Hackensack Water Company in 1924 after the enlargement of the Oradell reservoir. Courtesy Ford W. Quantmeyer, Sr., Harrington Park Historical Society

Before the competition of the railroads, the Hackensack river was a busy commercial artery as sailing vessels such as the one pictured here transported goods and raw materials along the river as far as the head of tidewater at New Milford (now Oradell). Courtesy Oradell Public Library

Jacob Van Buskirk's schooners, the Kate Laurence *and* General Grant *transported flour and feed from the Van Buskirk mill to markets in New York City. His house, pictured above, still stands on New Milford Avenue, formerly known as the Old Landing Road. Courtesy Oradell Public Library*

In 1851 Fort Lee was a small village of no more than thirty houses on the Hudson River at the foot of the Palisades. This early view depicts the approach to the landing which played an important part in Hudson River commerce many years before the American Revolution. Formerly known as Burdett's Ferry, the settlement took its present name from the revolutionary fort on the bluff overlooking the landing. National Anthropological Archives, Smithsonian Institution

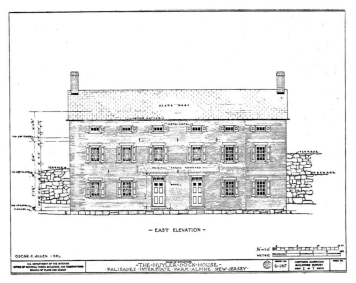

– EAST ELEVATION –

THE·HUYLER·DOCK·HOUSE·
PALISADES·INTERSTATE·PARK·ALPINE·NEW·JERSEY·

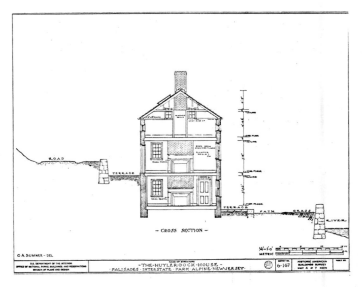

– CROSS SECTION –

THE·HUYLER·DOCK·HOUSE·
PALISADES·INTERSTATE·PARK·ALPINE·NEW·JERSEY·

The Huyler Dock House, built on the Hudson River just south of Alpine in the early 1800s, was a way-station for travelers, farmers, and commercial tradesmen. The remains of the building burned in 1973. Courtesy Historic American Buildings Survey, Library of Congress

This stock certificate from the collections of the Bergen County Historical Society identifies Albert G. Doremus of Hackensack as owner of ten shares in the Hackensack and Fort Lee Turnpike Company, incorporated in 1828. Courtesy Bergen County Historical Society

This locomotive was manufactured for the Hackensack and New York Railroad by Rogers Locomotive works in Paterson. Incorporated in 1856 it was not until 1861 that the railroad's tracks reached their northern terminus at Essex Street in Hackensack. The southern terminus was Erie Junction, a switching area a mile below Carlstadt where the trains exchanged cars with the Erie line. Later known as the Hackensack and New York Extension, the company was reorganized in 1874 as the New Jersey and New York Railroad. Running from Jersey City to Haverstraw, N.Y., the line was instrumental in opening the Pascack Valley to development. Courtesy of Newark Public Library

The Hackensack

BUILT BY THE ROGERS LOCOMOTIVE AND MACHINE WORKS IN 1860 FOR THE HACKENSACK AND NEW YORK RAILROAD.

This early print allegedly shows the first train of the Northern Railroad entering Englewood from the south, steaming past the farmers and cattle which the new technology would irrevocably displace. The artist's conception of Englewood considerably exaggerated its population. A developers' map filed in 1859 shows only three farm houses in the vicinity of the railroad. Courtesy Englewood Public Library

Montvale's Octagon House, was built circa 1850 by John Blauvelt, Jr., in the style popularized by Orson Squire Fowler. His publication, A Home for All, or the Gravel Wall and Octagon Mode of Building, was first published in 1848. During the following decade, houses were built in this style throughout the United States. According to their designer, octagonal houses were more economical to heat and provided more efficient use of floor space and ventilation. The house pictured here is now used by a real estate firm. Courtesy Pascack Historical Society

KNOW all men by these Presents that I David A
Demarest of Hering township in the County of Bergen
and State of New Jersey for and in Consideration
of the Sum of Seventy five Dollars to me in hand
Paid by Jacob P Debaun in the township of New
Berbadus and before the Sealing and Delivry of
these Presents, the Reciept Whereof I do hereby
Acknowledge and Sold, and by these Presents Do
Bergain and Sell unto the Said Jacob P Debaun
A Negro Girl Named Bat Aged fifteen years nine
months and Sixteen day, by these Presents Bargained
And Sold unto Jacob P Debaun or his Heirs and
Assigns for ever I the Said David A Demarest
for myself and for my heirs Executors and admynistrators
Do Warrent and for ever Defend the said Negro girl
unto the Said Jacob P Debaun his heirs and assigns
Against myself and my heirs Executors Admynistrators,
and Assigns Every Other person and persons What-
soever In Witness Whareof I have hereunto Sett
my hand and Seal the Eighteenth Day of
January In the year of Our Lord One thousand
Eight hundred and thirteen - - - - - - 1813
Signed Sealed and Delivered
In the Presents of us —
Halmeigh Van Wagonen   David ari demarest
Samuel Van Wagoner

Had the slave girl transferred in this bill of sale been born six years later, she would have been eligible for her freedom. The 1804 N.J. "Act for The Gradual Abolition of Slavery" held that girls born after July 4 of that year would be freed on their 21st birthday (boys at 25). Children born of slave women after 1804 had to be registered with the state by their owners as did Garrett Hopper of Saddle River in the winter of 1806. Courtesy Bergen County Historical Society

I Garret I Hopperd am an Inhabitant
of Saddle River and county of Bergen
and State of New Jersey had A
female child named Sarah Born of
a Slave the 17th of February
1806 —
                              Garret I Hopperd

BCHS 368B Doc #96

The small building to the right of the Huyler homestead, 50 County Road, Cresskill, has traditionally been regarded as slave quarters. Since the outbuilding is said to have been built in 1836 at the same time as the larger wing, it more likely accommodated Peter Huyler's free black servants. Census records show that in 1830, the Huylers held one slave, three black free men, and four free black females, two of whom were children. By 1840 he had no slaves at all. *Courtesy Howard W. Tallman, Cresskill Borough Historian*

Daniel Holsman

This portrait of state Senator Daniel Holsman was featured in an anti-war journal published during the midst of the Civil War. The editor referred to the Copperhead leader as "the distinguished champion of peace and of pure Democracy," and praised the series of resolutions he tried to push through the New Jersey Legislature in January 1863. Among the resolutions was one which referred to the Emancipation Proclamation as "a gross violation of the Constitution." From **The Old Guard**, *v. 2, 1864*

This document is one measure of the widespread support offered to the cause of the Union among Bergen citizens. The undersigned each contributed to a collection for the purchase of a "stand of colors" for the 22nd Regiment of New Jersey Volunteers. The flags were made by the Annin Company of Verona, New Jersey, at a cost of $200.00. *Courtesy Bergen County Historical Society*

chapter 3

The tidy back yards of Hackensack as they appeared after substantial new housing was added along Central Avenue to the New Jersey and New York Railroad tracks. In this view, looking southwest from Christ Church tower, the embankment and trestle of the New York Susquehanna and Western Railroad are clearly visible. Courtesy Johnson Free Public Library

Suburban Haven

When the Erie Railroad finished its Bergen County cut from Rutherford to Ridgewood in the early 1880s, the county's framework of railroads was complete. The tracks of the Northern and Southern Pacific pushing their way across the continent during much of the same period could not have made more of an impact on the territory they traversed. No longer would goods and produce be hauled in slow journeys to the rivers of Bergen on their way to market.

The railroads reached inland to the farms, the factories, the foundries and the mills. It was no accident that Cornelius A. Wortendyke, president of the Wortendyke mills, was also president of the New Jersey Midland Railway running through his town, now Midland Park. Even before the Civil War, real estate entrepreneurs had forseen the economic impact of the railroad. "Villa sites at Boiling Springs" were laid out in 1858 adjacent to the Erie Railroad in what is now Rutherford. Along the eastern shore, key backers of the Nothern Railroad acquired and surveyed the nucleus of present-day Englewood, and filed their map of building sites with the county clerk's office just two months before the first train arrived in 1859.

The era of the railroad was embraced with enthusiasm. In Bergen's northwestern corner, the coming of the railroad to quiet, agricultural Oakland in 1869 was an occasion for rejoicing. School was dismissed, cannons boomed, and Rodman Price, former New Jersey governor and the only Bergen resident ever to hold that office, came from his estate in Mahwah to add lustre to the events of the day. For better, or in the eyes of some, for worse, the ferment of change had reached to the far corners of Bergen County, and its old ways would be forever altered.

After the Civil War the pace of development quickened. Real estate interests and railroads combined in promotions designed to convince city dwellers, particularly New York businessmen, to relocate across the river. Special excursion trains deposited prospective suburbanites at isolated stations, where they would be welcomed with refreshments and, on occasion a brass band to lead the way to the property. "Land auctions" continued into the 1900s, setting the pattern for the county's configuration of separate communities, situated along the rail lines like beads on a string. Each was independent, autonomous and dedicated to home rule.

There were also forces at work within the cities which contributed to the building of these new suburban communities. Neighborhoods in Manhattan which had previously provided comfortable housing for upper and middle class families were becoming overcrowded and uncomfortable. Impoverished immigrants in great numbers were crowded into deteriorating housing, increasing the crime rate and straining facilities of health and sanitation. The wealthy might flee to Brooklyn or Harlem. Certainly many retained summer residences in the country, including Bergen County. City dwellers of more modest means; middle managers, white collar workers, found it necessary to live near their employment in the inner city.

The transportation revolution of the last half of the nineteenth century, however, brought about a profound change. The introduction of the horse car and then the steam locomotive extended the reach of the very dense urban core into the surrounding countryside. As Sam Bass Warner explains, the development of the electric street railway had even greater impact. Around Boston, disconnected towns such as Dorchester and Roxbury became "streetcar suburbs." Around New York the very nature of places such as Westchester and Bergen Counties were transformed.

The suburbs offered more than escape. Land auctioneer William Taylor's description of Bergenfield as a "booming village—a go ahead place," is typical of the sense of vitality found in these new communities. One is reminded of the "boosterism" that Daniel Boorstin has described in the growing cities of the American West during the same era. Bergen County suburbs may also be regarded, in another sense, as a more accessible frontier. Economic concentration and social stratification in the older cities made it unlikely that any but the most wealthy or well-connected would rise to positions of high social standing, but Englewood, Ridgewood and other suburban communities invited the establishment of new local elites. Bergen County developers promised a life of civilized and dignified refinement in which newcomers would live among the "best" and "most successful" New York businessmen. Competing real estate firms emphasized the spacious homes, the sometimes impressive railroad stations, the macadamized roads. Lives that for some may have seemed empty in the city were given meaning by their participation in the developing insti-

The **Nanuet**, the New Jersey and New York Railroad Company's locomotive, with tender and passenger cars at Wood-Ridge station circa 1887. Incorporated as the Hackensack and New York Railroad in 1856, the line's original route ran from Carlstadt to Hackensack, with a spur to Lodi. By 1870 tracks had been laid from Jersey City to Haverstraw, N.Y., with trains passing through Carlstadt, Wood-Ridge, Hasbrouck Heights, Hackensack, River Edge, New Milford, Oradell, Westwood, Hillsdale, and Park Ridge. Courtesy History of Wood-Ridge Committee

Demarest Station on the Northern Railroad of New Jersey was named for state Senator Ralph S. Demarest, one of the directors of the railroad. Designed in Richardsonian Romanesque style by J. Cleveland Cady, the station was built in 1872 of stone from the quarries of the Palisades. Cady, a well-known New York architect and designer of the original Metropolitan Opera House and one wing of the Museum of Natural History, had a summer home, "Cadiz," on the edge of the Palisades just north of the upper Closter dock at Alpine. Courtesy Demarest Public Library

tutions of new villages and boroughs, instilling community (and personal) pride.

Hospitals and charitable institutions were established to provide for the poor and the unfortunate. Fire and police protection grew out of town "improvement" or "protection" societies. During the years after 1876, the State Board of Education's renewed emphasis on educational improvement throughout the state certainly received a positive endorsement in many a Bergen County community. Libraries had their modest beginnings, frequently nurtured by women's associations and private philanthropy. Utilities and water supply systems were introduced according to the most modern standards of the day.

The sense of identity of place, nourished as it was by personal involvement in civic and cultural affairs, must have contributed to the so-called borough fever which infected the county in the mid 1890s. Reacting to an 1894 act of the state legislature which made it easier for boroughs to be established, more than a score of villages petitioned the state legislature for a borough charter. Local tensions were inevitable as prosperous suburban settlements grew up in the midst of rural farms. Rather than pay taxes to the township only to see a small portion of those funds returned to their neighborhood, citizens of such newly chartered boroughs could spend their own tax money as they wanted to, often for improved schools.

New suburban communities influenced the economy in numerous ways. From the beginning, for example, Bergen farmers had produced some crops for market, but now as New York, Newark and Jersey City and more local markets developed there was a shift to a more direct commercial identification. W. R. Boker of Creskill was putting his newly invented gas incubator to work hatching some two hundred thousand chickens per year, but the increase in poultry and dairy production also reflected the influx of factory workers who had to be fed. Some of these, to be sure, cultivated their own garden patches complete with scratching chickens. As the real estate value of their land soared, many farmers found themselves unable to make their farms pay as well as the speculators would. Gradually farm acreage fell from a peak of eighty-six thousand improved acres in 1860, to sixty-nine thousand in 1870, and forty-six thousand in 1900.

Industries grew as well. Some were based on the exploitation of local resources such as the stone quarried from the Palisades and used to pave New York's Broadway, or the clay which provided the raw material for several busy brickyards along the Hackensack River. A short-lived attempt was also made to reopen the Schuyler Copper Mine.

Manufacturing and commerce were more widespread and were encouraged by the availability of railroads to bring raw materials and carry out finished products. Much of Bergen's commercial establishment was still devoted to the manufacture and processing of textiles. Weaving mills, bleacheries and dye works employed thousands of workers of every conceivable ethnic background. Other significant Bergen industries were the production of paper and chemicals. The manufacture of carriages, chairs and other furniture continued from pre-Civil War days. Bicycles, baseballs and baby carriages were manufactured around Rutherford in the southern part of the county.

As part of the larger integrated industrial community of the New York metropolitan area, other manufacturers produced scores of specialty items and parts for larger assemblies. Among them were John B. Fortenbach's watch case factory in Carlstadt; the Peerless Manu-

Designed in a more conservative style, the Carlstadt Depot also reflected Victorian architectural conceits with its spindled fascia and bell-like cupola. The station was erected in 1891 by the New Jersey and New York Rail Road Company at their crossing on Paterson Plank Road in Carlstadt. The station sign atop the cupola was a weather vane paid for by private subscription. Similar cupolas adorned the company's stations in Hasbrouck Heights and at Central Avenue in Hackensack. Postcard courtesy New Jersey Historical Society

The village populations along the Hudson continued to rely upon steam and sail boats for transportation. Pictured here is the Pleasant Valley, one of the steam ferries operated by the Peoples Ferry Company between 1869 and 1888. The ferry ran from Canal Street in New York City to Fort Lee, with stops at Shadyside, Edgewater, and Pleasant Valley, towns which were later incorporated into the present Borough of Edgewater. Courtesy Edgewater Public Library

facturing Company of Ridgewood which produced soft rubber goods such as hoses and mats, and the Oakland Hair Works which processed materials for stuffing upholstered furniture and mattresses.

An expanding community of New York commuters, local factory workers and their families, supported a network of retail businesses and services. The local pharmacies, general stores and blacksmith shops with their pot-bellied stoves and cracker barrels around which town gossip swirled, reflected an old-fashioned spirit of community cohesiveness which would be lost in the more standardized and impersonal chain stores of a later era.

Hotels appeared in the wake of the railroads, in newly established towns and along the Palisades. Because of the fresh country air and the drama of the landscape, Bergen in the mid to late nineteenth century became a haven for tourists and vacationers who patronized such elegant hotels as the Palisades Mountain House, the Fort Lee Hotel and the Englewood House. City folk could also escape for the day to the Fort Lee Pavilion, the "Park on the Palisades," or to the rural delights of Hackensack. As the *New York Times* put it in July 1872, in addition to the "salubrious climate" and pleasant scenery, "some sport may be had too with dog and gun, and rod and line, more than would naturally be anticipated from the proximity of the locality to centers of trade and commerce." The images

conjured up by the writer must have been particularly appealing to readers steaming away the summer in their New York apartments: "the tired citizen, seeking for a brief escape from the heat and dust and everlasting cares of city life, will find few places that combine so many advantages." Despite such good reviews, however, the tourist business did not sustain itself and by the end of the century all but a few of the grand resort hotels had either burned or gone out of business.

Much has been written about the lifestyle of the Victorian era. From the opulence of the grand mansions such as the summer home of David B. Ivison in Rutherford or the Phelps mansion in Englewood, to comfortable suburban homes and tiny rural farmhouses; from the elegant formality of the engraved calling card to the relaxed atmosphere of a firemen's picnic; from the baseball craze to the bicycle boom, Bergen experienced the Victorian age in all of its diversity. With no densely populated urban area, the county escaped many of the problems that came with the slum neighborhoods of Newark and Paterson. However, with the mix of wealthy New York businessmen, more moderately successful white-collar commuters, local factory workers and shop-keepers, and small farmers, differences in tastes and social values were bound to arise. To some degree they were reflected in the vigorous efforts of groups such as the Women's Christian

Public and private carriages wait to pick up Erie Railroad commuters at Station Square in Rutherford at the turn of the century. Although the hacks have been replaced by *taxis, and family cars may no longer wait in the center of the square, debarking passengers such as those pictured at the right, still walk up Orient Way and Park Avenue at the* *completion of a day's work in New York City. Courtesy Meadowlands Museum*

Temperance Union which saw "demon rum" as a cause of moral decline. Much attention was focused on Fort Lee, where prize fights, dog fights and cock fights were common and "bookies" in local poolrooms took bets on the horse races at the Dundee Track in what is now Elmwood Park. Efforts to legalize gambling throughout the state in 1893, brought strong public reaction and dramatic Democratic Party losses at the polls in both state and county. Women's suffrage was another issue certain to sow dissention. Elizabeth Cady Stanton, one of the most vociferous leaders of the national movement, moved from New York to Tenafly in 1869, and proceeded to challenge the local election officials by demanding her right to vote.

Just as Dutch influence had helped to shape Bergen lifestyles in the colonial period, proximity to New York harbor, the entrepot for most immigrants arriving from overseas, assured that Bergen would have its newer immigrant influences. Individual immigrant families settled in every corner of the county, and became active participants in community life. In Woodridge in 1895, Anton Molinari, a recent immigrant of Italian ancestry and a successful entrepreneur, was elected mayor. Italians also settled in Lyndhurst, attracted by the shops of the Delaware Lackawana Railroad. In Carlstadt, a strong community of German immigrants took root. The Passaic Steam Laundry in North Arlington employed scores of

Chinese workers who lived in company houses on the premises. The English and Irish populations of Englewood, Leonia and the rest of what was known as the English Neighborhood were swelled with newcomers too. With all the variety and social change in the life of the late nineteenth century, however, singleness of purpose still prevailed in hard times. In the blizzard of 1888, and when a tornado ripped through Hackensack in 1895, Bergen communities pulled together in support.

According to historian Robert Wiebe, "the health of the nineteenth century community depended upon two closely related conditions: its ability to manage the lives of its members and the belief among its members that the community had such powers." In the decades after the Civil War as new suburban communities sprang up among old farming villages, these elements of stability were subjected to new and hitherto unfamiliar tensions. The turn-of-the-century and later the influence of the World War would propel Bergen County and its people into an exciting if unpredictable future.

53

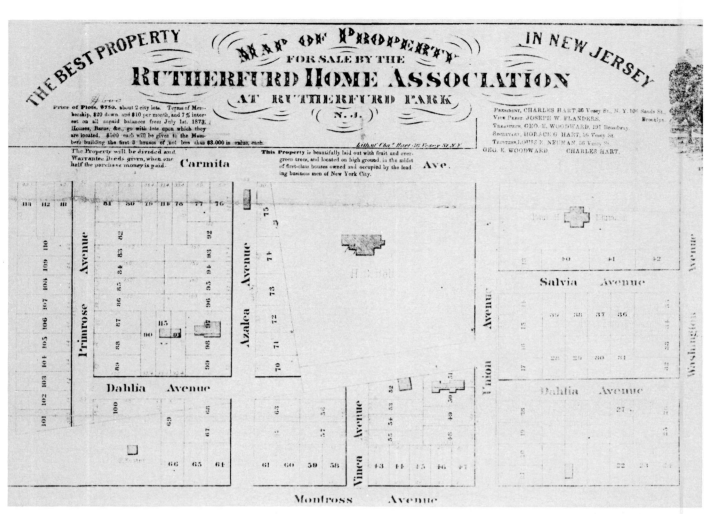

The Rutherford Home Association was typical of real estate developers active in Bergen County following the Civil War. The house indicated on plots 50 and 51 Union Avenue was purchased by Fairleigh Dickinson University in 1955 and is now known as Kingsland House on the university's Rutherford campus. Courtesy Special Collections, Alexander Library, Rutgers University

Miss Eleanor Van Gelder, one of the first teachers in Edgewater's one-room school, was hired in 1882 for $30.00 per month. Thirteen years later she was appointed principal, a post she would hold until her retirement. Although the small wooden school and its brick successor were demolished in 1935, Miss Van Gelder's educational legacy to Edgewater survives in the Eleanor Van Gelder School on Undercliff Avenue. Courtesy Edgewater Public Library

Passengers wait at Oradell Depot to board a train on the New Jersey and New York line. The building partly hidden by the station is the Hotel Delford, a popular vacation spot for summer visitors who enjoyed fishing, swimming and canoeing on the Hackensack River nearby. Photograph by William King, courtesy Bergen County Historical Society

Principal Ralph S. Maugham stands with the graduating class of Tenafly's first elementary school, a two-story brick building on the corner of Clinton Avenue and Tenafly Road. Two of the boys are wearing the military caps of the Rethmore Boys Brigade, a company of the United Boys Brigades of America, a quasi-military organization which encouraged the practice of military arts. The Tenafly unit drilled at Rethmore Hall, for many years a community center which at one time served as a fresh-air camp for underprivileged city children. The Reformed Church in Oradell also sponsored a Boy's Brigade unit which met in the church parlor. The popularity of the movement was gradually eroded after 1910 by the organization of the Boy Scouts of America. Courtesy Virginia Mosley, Tenafly Borough Historian

ANNUAL EXAMINATION

FOR

First and Second Grade Diplomas in the Public Schools

OF BERGEN COUNTY, FOR THE YEAR 1889.

John Terhune, County Superintendent.

June 3d, Morning. *ORTHOGRAPHY and ETYMOLOGY. First and Second Grades.*

1. What knowledge is necessary in order to pronounce a word correctly? To spell it correctly? To write it correctly? To analyze it correctly? To understand it correctly?
2. Define Diphthong, Digraph, Alphabetic Equivalent, Vowel, Consonant.
3. Write ten words each containing a digraph and mark the character representing the elementary sound.
4. Indicate by diacritical marks the power of "a" in the following words: made, man, mark, mast, what, many, talk, Aaron.
5. Give rules for spelling: "reference"; referred; peaceable; believing; varied.
6. Analyze etymologically: confidant; objection; circumlocution; impartial; opposition.
7. Write euphonic variations of the following prefixes: ad-, con-, sub-, in-.
8. Show the root, radical, prefix and suffix in the following words: intercession; conclusion; incorporate; inaccurate; confidently; ambition.

9, 10. Desuetude, turgid, armistice, mortise, cedilla, satiate, obeisance, buoyant, indictment, veranda, nieces, prairie, roguish, nursling, privileges, recommend, preparation, accommodate, awful, trisyllable.

June 3d, Afternoon. *READING.* *Second Grade.*

1. What do punctuation marks indicate?
2. When is a syllable long? Short? Neutral?
3. Give five rules for the use of elocutionary pauses.
4. Upon what does the length of a pause depend?
5. What are the elements of vocal expression?
6. What is stress? Name the three principal varieties.
7. Define and illustrate *simple* and *compound* inflections.
8. In what three ways may a word be rendered emphatic?
9. What is the old-fashioned plan of teaching reading?
10. What general rule do good readers observe?

June 3d, Afternoon. *SCIENCE OF COMMON THINGS. First Grade.*

1. Why is a hollow tube of metal stronger than the same quantity of metal as a solid rod?
2. What is weight? Why will a ball of lead weigh more than a ball of cotton of the same size?
3. How slight a declivity is sufficient to give a running motion to water? On what principle are we enabled to conduct water underground through irregular tubes?
4. What quantity of mineral matter is generally contained in comparatively pure natural waters?
5. Why does the body of a drowned person rise and float upon the surface several days after death?
6. What is the difference between a thermometer and a barometer?
7. How is sound produced? What solids are among the best conductors of sound?
8. How can most of the stories in respect to the so-called "haunted houses" be explained?
9. Why is it frequently cooler after a rain?
10. What are the conditions necessary in order that we may see a rainbow?

June 4th, Morning. *GRAMMAR. First and Second Grades.*

1. What is language? English Grammar? An idea? A thought? A sentence?
2. How are sentences divided as to form? How as to meaning? Give an example of each.
3. Diagram or analyze the following sentence and parse the italicized words:
   "Reputation *is* what we seem, *but* character *is* what *we* are."

4 and 5. Write a letter to the District Clerk of your school district, telling him about the Arbor Day exercises.

6. Name in their order the different parts of a letter.

7 and 8. Write ten abbreviations and ten contractions. What is the difference between an abbreviation and a contraction? Use don't and doesn't in sentences.

9. Correct the following: Please except my thanks. How did the news effect him? Will you learn me to play chess? I remain yours respectively. She has laid down to rest. Taste of this fruit. Put the vase up on to the shelf. You hadn't ought to use any unnecessary words. A strait connects them together. Milk is healthy for children. He had information of the lungs.
10. Name the parts of speech and the properties of each. No definitions.

(Mark the average in writing from the letter in question 4 and 5.)

June 4th, Afternoon. *GEOGRAPHY.* *First and Second Grades.*

1. In what County is Paterson? Newark? Jersey City? Long Branch? Trenton?
2. Name the Territories and the Capital of each.
3. Draw figure representing the zones of the earth. Write the names of the zones, width, and the circles bounding them on each; also your christian name on the zone in which you live.
4. Name ten capes on the eastern coast of the United States?
5. Name ten principal seaports of the United States.
6. Name the waters through which you would sail on the shortest voyage from Baltimore to Bombay.
7. Of what is the island of Great Britain composed? Name the waters surrounding it, and the principal cities.
8. Write a short description of Australia.
9. For what is France and its capital particularly noted?
10. Name the government of each of the countries of South America.

June 5th, Morning. *ARITHMETIC.* *First and Second Grades.*

1. Express ⅛ of one-hundredth as a decimal. Find the product of the two smallest decimals that can be expressed by the figures 0, 0, 9, and 3.
2. Find three numbers less than 125 which are multiples of both 12 and 18.
3. $\frac{1}{2} - .05 + \frac{1}{4} + .5 - .025 + \frac{3}{4} - \frac{1}{8} + 2.03 - .01 = ?$
4. Thos. Jones & Co. purchased from Samuel Smith, of Englewood: 6984 lbs. coal a. $4.85 a ton, 837½ lbs. beef a. $6.43 per cwt., 4750 envelopes a $1.37 per M., 421⅛ bush. oats a. 27½ cts. a bushel, 3250 ceiling lath a. 18½c. a hundred. Make out and receipt bill as clerk.
5. There is a number that will divide every one of the numbers 637, 504, 756, and 1001. What is it?
6. How many pints of water in a tank 11 ft. by 7 ft., and 3 feet deep?
7. How high should wood four feet long be piled on a sleigh 10 feet long to make two cords?
8. A bridge 132 yards long and 18 feet wide is covered with plank 2½ inches thick. Find the value of the plank at $18.50 per thousand.
9. A pint of water is put into a gallon of milk: what per cent. of the mixture is water?
10. A man invested $2,400 in a publishing business, and at the end of 2½ years he withdrew $2,940, being investment and profits. What annual rate of interest did his investment pay?
11. Face of note, $2,500. Time, 90 days. Rate of discount, 9 per cent. Date of note, June 3. Date of discount, August 13. Find the proceeds.
12. In arranging the terms of a partnership, A has a note of $460 not bearing interest, B has a similar note of $345 but having three times as long to run. A is willing to allow $300 for B's note. How much should B allow for A's?

(Second Grade solve the first ten examples, and First Grade last ten.)

June 5th, Afternoon. *PHYSIOLOGY.* *First and Second Grades.*

1. Name the three important cavities of the skeleton. Locate the following: Humerus; Clavicle; Sternum; Patella; Tarsus.
2. Name five bad habits in eating which cause indigestion
3. Name some uses of the skin; hair; nails.
4. Name five important digestive organs, and five digestive fluids.
5. Describe the heart. Why does the heart beat?
6. How are the arteries and veins connected?
7. What effect has bad air and violent exercise upon the heart? What is the effect of unwholesome food? Too little sleep? Improper clothing?
8. What causes malaria? What are the effects of wearing tight clothing and small shoes?
9. State five ways in which the eyes may be injured. Name the parts of the ear.
10. Describe that part of the body with which we think.

June 6th, Morning. *ALGEBRA.* *First and Second Grades.*

1. What determines the degree of a term? Write a Homogeneous Polynomial.
2. $\frac{a+1}{a-1} \div \frac{a-1}{a+1} = ?$
3. Given $\frac{5x}{9} = x - \frac{2x-56}{3}$, to find x.
4. Find the value of v, w, x, y, and z in the following equations:

$$\begin{aligned} v+w+x+y&=10\\ v+w+x+z&=11\\ v+w+y+z&=12\\ v+x+y+z&=13\\ w+x+y+z&=14 \end{aligned}$$

5. Given $\left\{\begin{array}{l} 3x+2y=23 \\ x+4y=21 \end{array}\right\}$ to find x and y.
   Solve this by all three methods of elimination.
6. Find three numbers, such that the first with ⅓ of the other two, the second with ¼ of the other two, or the third with 1-5 of the other two, shall be equal to 25.
7. Given $x - \frac{1}{2}\sqrt{x} = \sqrt{x^2 - x}$ to find x.
8. Expand $(x-1)^6$ by the binominal theorem.
9. What is the price of oranges when eight more in a dollar's worth would lower the price five cents a dozen?
10. A cistern is to be built in the form of a cylinder capable of holding 9,000 gallons; and its depth is to be equal to its diameter. Find the dimensions.

June 6th, Afternoon. *HISTORY AND CONSTITUTION. First and Second Grades.*

1. With what design did Columbus sail? Give his reason for this design, and state what was much wanted.
2. State who founded Rhode Island and what led to it. Where and by whom was New Jersey settled? Why so named?
3. Name the principal wars previous to the Revolution, with one important battle in each; and the names of the generals on both sides.
4. What battles of the Revolution were fought in New Jersey? When and where was Gen. Washington first inaugurated President?
5. When and where was the first blood shed in the Revolution and in the War of Secession? What disaster happened to the American and German men-of-war recently? Where did it occur, and why were they there?
6. Of what does Congress consist? When will the next session of Congress meet? How many Senators will there be?
7. What are the duties of the President?
8. How are new States admitted?
9. What shall the United States guarantee to every State in the Union?
10. How is the Vice President chosen? Who were Vice Presidents during Cleveland's administration?

June 7th, Morning. *BOOK-KEEPING.* *First and Second Grades.*

1. Write a negotiable note bearing interest.
2. Samuel Smith gives James Bush a draft at 60 days sight on Thomas Thorn, Buffalo, N. Y., for mdse.
   Make Journal entry for each person named in the draft.
3. If the Dr. and Cr. sides of Bills Payable account are unequal, which side must be the larger and why?
4. When will Bills Receivable account balance?
5. Upon closing the Ledger, I find the Dr. side of Profit and Loss account the larger. Has my business been prosperous or not? Why?
6. After closing my books, to which account must I refer for my Resources and Liabilities?
7. Give order of closing a double-entry set of books.
8. James Edwards, of Paterson, N. J., bought of Edward Coombs, 10 bbls. flour a. $5.75, 15 sacks salt a. $1.80; and gave his check on the First National Bank of his city to Edward Coombs in payment.
   Make bill and write check.
9. Make Journal entries for James Edward and Edward Coombs.
10. What is the difference between a trial-balance and a balance-sheet?

June 7th, Afternoon. *MENSURATION.* *First and Second Grades.*

1. A field in the form of a rectangle is 15 chains long and 40 rods wide; how many acres does it contain?
2. Find the cost of plastering the walls and ceiling of a room 21 feet long, 12 feet wide, and 9 feet high, with 4 openings, each 8 feet by 4 feet, at 12 cents per square yard.
3. A box made of 2-inch plank is 3 feet 4 inches long, 2 feet 8 inches wide, and 1 foot 6 inches high. It has no lid. How much will it cost to cover the box completely, inside and outside, with gold leaf at $2 per square foot?
4. If the scale on a map is 4 miles to the inch, how many acres are there in a township which is represented by a square whose side is 1¾ inches?
5. A tree 72 feet high is broken 20 feet from the ground. How far from the foot will the top reach?
6. A farmer owns a field in the form of an isosceles triangle, the equal sides being each 100 rods, and the other side 160 rods. Find the area of the field.
7. A land-roller 3½ feet in diameter has its surface painted at a cost of 27 cents per square yard, its length being 14 feet. Find cost.
8. The difference between the diameter and the circumference of a circle is 10 feet. Find the diameter.
9. How many bushels of corn can be put into a corn-crib 9 feet square at the bottom, 12 feet square at the top, and 8 feet high?
10. How many square feet in the surface of a foot-ball 1 foot in diameter?

A sample of the battery of tests which confronted Bergen County teachers seeking certification in 1889. By state law, candidates for a First Grade Diploma (teaching certificate) were required to be eighteen years old with two year's teaching experience. Marked on a scale of 100, no candidate was licensed whose average fell below seventy. Courtesy Bergen County Historical Society

In 1804 Jacob Van Winkle donated a section of his land in what is now Lyndhurst, for the erection of a schoolhouse, claiming rent of one peppercorn per year upon demand. The "Little Red Schoolhouse" pictured here is the third such structure to stand upon the River Road site. Built in 1893, the one-room school operated continuously until the summer of 1982, and has served as an historic museum operated by the Meadowlands Museum, based in Rutherford. *Courtesy Newark Public Library*

In 1894 Tenafly became one of twenty-six towns incorporated during the so-called borough fever which swept Bergen County. This photograph of Tenafly's first official family was taken January 25, 1895. In addition to the mayor and council, the group includes the borough clerk, assessor, commissioners of appeals, three marshalls and four members of the Board of Health. *Courtesy Virginia Mosley, Tenafly Borough Historian*

Private alternatives to public education included elementary day schools, operated by educated women in their homes in the "dame school" tradition of colonial days. In 1888 Miss Amelia Haring organized such a school where, in addition to teaching the 3 R's, "efforts were made to cultivate the moral and religious natures of children and to instill into their youthful minds high ideas of correct deportment." Here Miss Haring's pupils pose before her father's handsome Italianate residence on the corner of Magnolia and Hillside Avenues in Tenafly. Dr. Haring was a gifted and well-beloved physician whose published reminiscences, Floating Chips, *captured the flavor of life in Bergen County's Northern Valley during the 1800s. Courtesy Virginia Mosley, Tenafly Borough Historian*

Ramsey firemen in dress parade uniforms ornament their fire house, erected circa 1900 on land donated by Lavinia Dater. Firemen and their friends were free to shoot pool on the second floor of the building which was also used for meetings of the governing body and other groups. The department's first fire engine was purchased secondhand from the Rutherford Fire Department in 1898. Courtesy Home and Store News

G. Bogert, charter member of Edgewater's Fire Department, organized in 1893. Courtesy Edgewater Public Library

Horizontal chemical tanks (astride the rear axle) date this piece of Park Ridge fire equipment to the 1880s or later. The tanks visible on the truck contained a solution of sodium bi-carbonate and water, activated by the release of concentrated sulphuric acid. Firemen replenished the chemical tanks from *water buckets hanging along the ladder racks. In the later nineteenth century, chemical fire fighting equipment was common in New England and in New Jersey where it served either as an alternative or as a supplement to the more expensive "steamers." Courtesy Pascack Historical Society*

Until the arrival of the sophisticated siren, local firemen were summoned by the clamor of an iron railroad or trolley rail, bent in a ring and hammered with a heavy metal implement. This early Tenafly fire alarm was duplicated in communities all over the county. One still stands outside Paramus Fire Department No. 4 on Farview Avenue. Courtesy Virginia Mosley, Tenafly Borough Historian

Hackensack Hospital was founded in 1888 largely through the efforts of a local physician, David St. John, supported by William M. Johnson, prominent lawyer and politician. A nurses training school was added during *the first ten years of the hospital's existence. In 1897 the hospital treated 462 patients and made a profit of $400 on an income of $5,200. Courtesy Johnson Free Public Library*

The chimes still ring from the Johnson Public Library tower clock on Main Street in Hackensack, as they have for more than three quarters of a century. Pictured here is the original building built of Belleville stone in 1901, largely with substantial gifts of land and money from William M. Johnson, New Jersey state senator, who also contributed generously to the addition of a new wing in 1915. Extensively remodeled and enlarged in 1967, the building now boasts a new entrance on Moore Street, and serves all of southern Bergen County as an Area Reference Library. In a tasteful blend of the old and the new, Johnson Library still presents its Gothic facade to the Main Street passerby. Courtesy Johnson Free Public Library

The former Bergen County Courthouse, successor of many buildings which housed the county courts and jail after New Barbadoes was detached from Essex County in 1709 to become part of Bergen County. After the courthouse was burned in a British raid in 1780, court was convened in a variety of locations, returning to The Green in Hackensack in 1819. Pictured here circa 1900, the building was demolished in 1912 for the construction of the present edifice. Courtesy Johnson Free Public Library

Thirty-five years after the Schuyler Copper Mine had been abandoned in 1865, The Arlington Copper Company was incorporated for $2,500,000 in what was the final attempt to extract ore from the North Arlington lode. Although the company spared no expense in the construction of a mill, roasting ovens, and leaching tanks, their endeavors remained unsuccessful, and in 1902 the Schuyler mine became the province of generations of spelunkers and adventurous boys. Bergen County directors of the ill-fated corporation included Henry C. Bell and William McKenzie from the Rutherford area. Courtesy Bergen County Historical Society

COPPER.

Excursion to the Mines and Works of the Arlington Copper Company.

At the request of a number of interested parties, a public invitation is hereby extended to all interested, free of charge, to visit on Saturday, November 24, the mines and extensive mineral deposits owned by this company, and the copper reduction works of 125 tons daily capacity, capable of producing refined copper at a very low cost, now in process of erection, all of which are located at Arlington, N. J., eight miles from New York City. The cars land you on the property.

Six thousand feet of underground drifts and tunnels have been run, and extensive development work completed. Experts estimate **5,000,000 tons** of copper ore now in sight ready for mining and milling.

The train will leave on Greenwood Lake Branch of the Erie Railroad at 1:30 o'clock, from Chambers Street Ferry; returning, arrive at New York at 6:30 P. M., or sooner. if necessary. Guides will be in attendance, and an interesting and instructive afternoon will be spent reviewing the commercial and historical features of this property, which has been widely talked about. Mining experts and the mining fraternity are especially invited.

All desiring to attend, apply to the

**ARLINGTON COPPER COMPANY,
Room 38, No. 2 Wall Street,   New York City.**

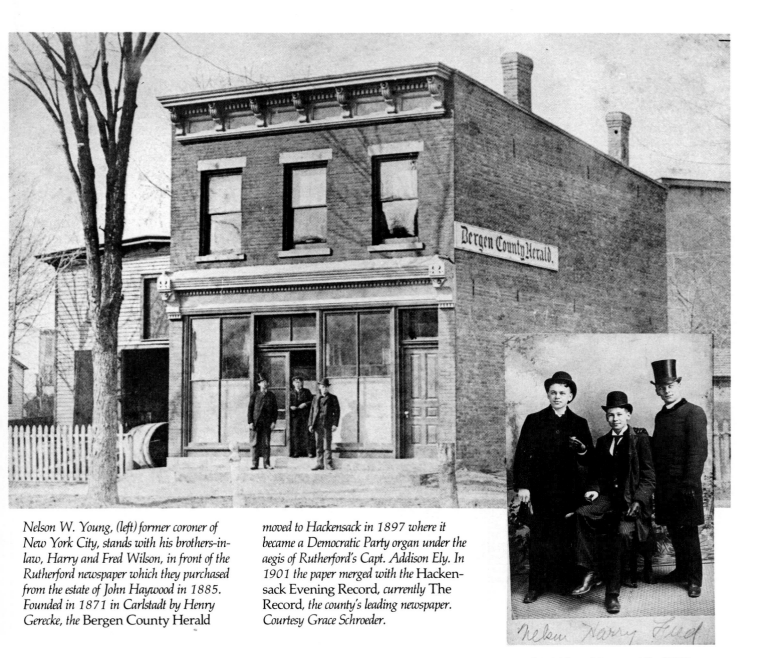

Nelson W. Young, (left) former coroner of New York City, stands with his brothers-in-law, Harry and Fred Wilson, in front of the Rutherford newspaper which they purchased from the estate of John Haywood in 1885. Founded in 1871 in Carlstadt by Henry Gerecke, the Bergen County Herald moved to Hackensack in 1897 where it became a Democratic Party organ under the aegis of Rutherford's Capt. Addison Ely. In 1901 the paper merged with the Hackensack Evening Record, currently The Record, the county's leading newspaper. Courtesy Grace Schroeder.

From left, Nelson, Harry and Fred Wilson, circa 1885, Rutherford's budding journalists. After a stint at the Buffalo Evening News, Nelson became a physician and was the first to treat President McKinley, wounded by an assassin. Harry also abandoned a journalistic career to become a minister and educator in Boonton. Fred remained a newspaperman and later became editor of the Police Gazette. Courtesy Grace Schroeder

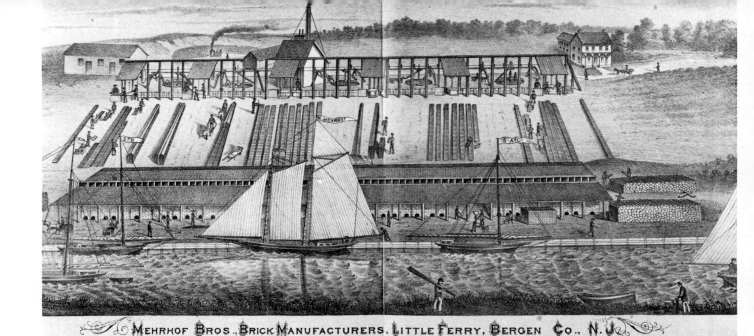

MEHRHOF BROS., BRICK MANUFACTURERS, LITTLE FERRY, BERGEN CO., N.J.
SHIPPERS AND WHOLESALE DEALERS IN BEST QUALITY MOLDING SAND FOR FRONT AND COMMON BRICK. — SUPERIOR QUALITY POTTER'S CLAY FURNISHED TO ORDER.

In 1867 the Mehrhof brothers purchased the brick yard near Little Ferry which had been in operation for the previous five years with little success. Under their direction the business grew into what Clayton's History described as "next to largest in the United States." In 1882 they were producing over two million bricks per year from the area's abundant clay deposits, shipping them down the Hackensack River to New York, Newark, Paterson and Providence, on their private fleet of schooners. The firm continued until well into the twentieth century. From Walker, Atlas

Finished Belgian blocks designed for paving New York City streets appear in the left foreground, dramatically high-lighting the destructive quarrying operations which threatened the Palisades during the last quarter of the nineteenth century. In 1900, twelve thousand cubic yards of rock were blasted away daily from Fort Lee bluff. In the last decade of the century, the New Jersey State Federation of Women's Clubs conducted an intensive campaign to preserve the Palisades. Their efforts were rewarded in 1900 by the establishment of the Palisades Interstate Park Commission, a joint endeavor by the states of New Jersey and New York. With public and private funding (J. P. Morgan contributed $125,000) the commission purchased quarry after quarry until 1909 when the Palisades were finally secured from commercial exploitation. This photograph is from the collection of Karl B. Lamb, whose family was active in the crusade to save the Palisades. Courtesy Howard Tallman, Cresskill Borough Historian

A drawing of the Hudson River Chemical and Dye-Wood Company as it appeared in 1875. Although the company's New Jersey incorporation record of 1869 locates the firm at Bull's Ferry, Hudson County, its true location was for many years at Shadyside, now a section of Edgewater. Dyewood was a heavy reddish wood imported from Central America for use as a dyestuff. In this birds-eye view, the busy locomotives in the background with their alternating plumes of steam, constitute an artistic fiction, since there were no railroads in the area at that time. In the foreground the well-documented steam ferry, Pleasant Valley, is making a scheduled stop at the Shadyside landing. Courtesy New York Historical Society

As early as 1857 the Collignon brothers, Nicholas and Claudius, had set up a chair factory on the Hackensack River on what is now Westwood Avenue at the boundary of Old Tappan. A third brother, Adam, later started a similar firm in River Vale. Among them, the Collignon brothers held ten patents for an assortment of folding chairs which they manufactured for clients the world over, including deck chairs for the Cunard Line and other steamship companies. The photograph, circa 1875, shows Claudius, center in the dark suit and necktie, perhaps flanked by his brothers; the trio surrounded by workmen from the chair factory. Courtesy Old Tappan Public Library

Folding deck chair. From Walker, Atlas

The building at the left in this photograph was originally Ramsey's first church, erected circa 1826 by a Dutch Reformed congregation. Fifty years later John Young Dater purchased the building and moved it to his Main Street property to become a show room and depository for the wagons, buggys and sleighs manufactured by his wheelwright and blacksmith shop. A Ramsey businessman and politician, John Y. Dater served in the New Jersey Legislature during the Civil War. In 1882 Dater sold the complex to M. B. De Yoe, who remodelled the buildings into a row of stores. Courtesy Home and Store News

Employees of the Triphammer Foundry exhibit some of the agricultural implements manufactured at this important Saddle River site. Founded by John and David Ackerman in the early 1800s, the foundry was acquired after the Civil War by William W. Packer who had previously operated a saw mill and basket factory in the 1840s off West Saddle River Road. Courtesy Paramus Historical and Preservation Society

The land continued to support many Bergen County families. Members of the Zabriskie-Westervelt family posed with their animals at the David Zabriskie farm on what is now Grant Avenue in Oradell. Because of their great strength, oxen were frequently used for clearing land, hauling or plowing. Courtesy Oradell Public Library

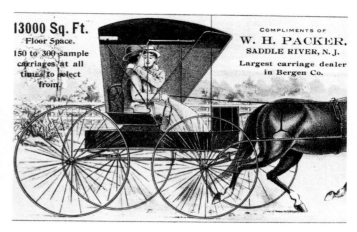

Milton Packer poses with his horse and racing sulky, perhaps on his way to a meet at the Ho-Ho-Kus Race Track, where he was a member of the Ho-Ho-Kus Driving Club. The house behind him at one time belonged to the Woodruff family who operated the foundry from circa 1840 through the Civil War. Courtesy Saddle River Historical Committee

In the late 1800s the Packers added to their own locally-produced iron products a variety of items from other manufacturers supplying the horse and buggy era. In 1900 their wagon warehouse was the largest in the county, if not the state, serving customers in Rockland, Passaic, Sussex and Morris Counties as well. In 1911 William H. Packer operated a dealership for Flanders automobiles; later he sold Studebakers. Courtesy Saddle River Historical Committee

Men (and boys) employed in Hinners's lumber products mill which was operated in the late 1800s by Edo H. Hinners, first mayor of Edgewater. Employees in the first row display tools of their trade, circular saw blades and a hammer. The business continued into the 1920s as a building supply house. Courtesy Edgewater Public Library

In addition to manufacturing "fine cigars," Theodore Muehling carried "a large variety of smoking and chewing tobaccos and smokers' articles in general." A native of Saxony, Mr. Muehling came to the United States in 1849. He moved to Park Avenue in Rutherford in 1893 after operating in Carlstadt for twenty-years. In 1895 his staff included twelve assistants, not including the traditional cigar-store Indian. Courtesy Meadowlands Museum

The Hopkins and Dickinson bronze and lock works was Mahwah's first industry, established circa 1872 by A. B. Darling who held a sizeable investment in the New York City firm. Established on thirty acres on the Ramapo River between the Darling residence and Valley Road, the firm employed over one hundred workers in busy times, recruiting area farmers' sons as well as Irish immigrants from New York City. After the firm moved to Newark in 1881, the foundry buildings were converted to a silo and a storage barn on the Darling estate.

Interior of Rutherford's Park Pharmacy on Depot Square circa 1900. In 1895 proprietor Frank E. Hatch advertised a full line of drugs, chemicals and patent medicines; soda water, stationery and perfumes. Notice the soda fountain at left, and in the middle of the aisle, a steam radiator. Courtesy Meadowlands Museum

Colonel A. G. Demarest moved from Closter to Tenafly to establish this general store in the early 1870s. Conveniently located on Highwood Avenue near the railroad station, the store has catered to Tenafly's needs, domestic and professional, for more than one hundred years. This early photograph includes the well which, as wells have done from biblical times, provided a convenient meeting-place for the townspeople. Demarest's wares included feed and coal; groceries, candy, liquor, hardware, housewares, building supplies and dress goods. Courtesy Virginia Mosley, Tenafly Borough Historian

A roof-top spectator watches the photographer of Lloyd McNomee's general store in Oakland circa 1890. Although the building has been considerably altered during the years, its handsome Mansard roof may still be recognized at 384 Ramapo Valley Road in Oakland. *Courtesy Oakland Historical Society*

In 1896 W. D. Kingsland's funeral parlor was located at 510 Main Street in Hackensack, telephone no. 45A. He advertised: "open day and night." *Courtesy Johnson Free Public Library*

Mrs. D. Brown's Cleaning House and Dye Works was in Ridgewood near the Moore Building. The policeman has been tentatively identified as James Houlihan, one of three police officers in 1897. A hand-lettered sign in the window announces that ladies may leave their white kid gloves for cleaning. *Courtesy* The Ridgewood NEWSpapers

Dinty Grady's Hack

One Sunday morning early, Pat Finn and Mary Hurley,
Fred Kronin and Tom Daley, myself and my boy Jack,
And nobby Dinty Grady with his liv'ry coat and cady,
He drove each gent and lady in his yellow-painted hack.

Chorus: Oh, my pony, go 'long, my pony!
       He is a pacer, the fastest on the track:
       Oh, my pony, go 'long, my pony!
       He'll beat 2:40 pulling Dinty Grady's hack.

And when we crossed the ferry, all feeling very merry
From drinking port and sherry, the tide was rather slack;
And seagulls by the million were dancing a cotillion
While passing the pavilion we drove Dinty Grady's hack.

Repeat chorus.

We reached our destination, the horse in perspiration;
We took a long vacation, in far-off Hackensack!
And there we picked the flowers, unmindful of the hours,
Until the falling showers drove us into Dinty's hack.

Repeat chorus.

Drivers and their rigs in the yard of Lawrence
O. Smith's Boarding and Livery Stable on
Erie Avenue near the railroad station in
Rutherford. In 1892 Smith advertised horses
and carriages available at all hours, and
"orders for the late trains promptly attended
to." Photo courtesy Meadowlands Museum

An old folksong recalls the fun of a carriage
ride from New York City to the rural delights
of Hackensack. Song courtesy of Anne Lutz
from the recollections of Mrs. Russell Knichel
of Mahwah and Anna T. Lehlbach, East
Orange. The first and third stanzas were
previously published in the Newsletter of the
New Jersey Folklore Society.

Franz Fritsch's tavern on Hackensack Street in Wood-Ridge continued the traditions of hospitality established at that location by the first tavern in Wood-Ridge. Originally known as the Windisch Hotel, the hostel was operated for many years by Wilhelm Gleitzman, giving rise to the local designation of the area as Wilhelm's Hoehe (William's Heights). Fritsch's license fee of $149.06 in 1895 provided the newly incorporated Borough of Wood-Ridge with its first revenue. The tavern was operated through the 1930s by Otto Niederer who married Fritsch's daughter, the young lady second from left in this turn-of-the-century photograph. Courtesy History of Wood-Ridge Committee

Tenafly householders would wake to the chink and rattle of milk bottles, heralding another delivery from Martha Hanvey's dairy on De Mott Street. The patient horse soon learned the route, stopping at one customer's house after another without direction from the milkman. Courtesy Virginia Mosley, Tenafly Borough Historian

The Carlstadt Bottling Co. Charles Koegel, Woodridge, N. J.

Although the Carlstadt Bottling Works took its name from a neighboring borough, the operation had been located on the east side of Hackensack Street in Wood-Ridge since before 1900. After Charles Koegel purchased the business in 1909, he moved it to a more convenient location next to his tavern across the street. William Peter Brewing Company was a Hoboken concern. Postcard courtesy History of Wood-Ridge Committee

The Englewood House, incorporated in 1866, was typical of new hotel ventures occasioned by the advent of the railroads in Bergen County. Guests were likely to include prospective village residents, transients, and summer visitors who were attracted by the fresh country air and the clear water of a nearby bountiful spring. Located on Engle Street two blocks from the train depot, the hotel served as the center of village social life into the 1890s. J. A. Humphrey, an Englewood contemporary who enjoyed its home-like atmosphere, called it the "real estate exchange of Englewood." After serving as a school building for a number of years around the turn of the century, the hotel was finally demolished circa 1907 for the construction of an elementary school. Courtesy Library of Congress

"Victorian Gates," Peter Ackerman's handsome residence, once stood near the corner of East Ridgewood Avenue and Paramus Road. Decorative ironwork graced the mansard roof and the tower with its panoramic view. A spacious veranda surrounded two sides of the building. Interior details included eleven fireplaces and an entrance hall of white marble. Peter Ackerman was a member of the New Jersey Assembly during the 1880s, and first president of the First National Bank of Ridgewood. Courtesy Newark Public Library

Fort Lee Park Hotel and Pavilion.

These new and magnificent Buildings, in a romantic Park of forty acres in extent, are now open, and offer to the public, the most desirable Summer resort in the vicinity of New York. Located at the beginning of the Palisades, a varied and extended view of the Hudson River and New York Bay, is afforded. Among the many natural attractions, are wild scenery, grand old Trees, Rocky Cliffs, Rustic Walks and Fine Lawns, while elegant Carriage Roads, Fine Bathing Houses, and excellent Boating facilities, increase the attractions of the place.

Large Restaurants, capable of seating one thousand persons at one time, fine Bowling Alleys, and Billiard Room, offer to the transient guests every means of comfort and amusement, while the new Hotel has accommodations for permanent guests, unsurpassed.

The Grounds and Pavilion, are illuminated by Weston's Electric Light. Conterno's Military Band, with Herr Adam Seifert, Solo Cornetist, gives Grand Concerts each Afternoon and Evening during the season.

Mr. George L. Huggins, of the Cosmopolitan Hotel, is the proprietor of the new Hotel and Pavilion, and under his able management, guests are assured of most satisfactory attention to their comfort and enjoyment.

TIME TABLE
Steamboats PLEASANT VALLEY, HAMPTON & FORT LEE
LEAVE DAILY AND SUNDAYS,

Canal Street,	24th Street,	34th Street.
9 A. M. to 9 P. M. (Hourly.)	9.10 A. M. to 9.10 P. M. (Hourly)	9.15 A. M. to 8.15 P. M. (Hourly.)

Boats Return at 8, 10, 11 A. M. 12 M. 1, 2, 3, 4. 5.30, 6.30. 8, 10,15 P. M.

Excursion Tickets 25 Cents.

Manhattanville Ferry, (foot 125th St.) every hour from
7.30 A. M. to 10.30 P. M.
FERRIAGE 10 CENTS.

According to Clayton's History of Bergen County, *thousands of excursionists found their way to Fort Lee, many arriving on the steam ferries which docked hourly during the summer months. The Fort Lee Park Hotel and Pavilion, a resort hotel and amusement center, was situated directly on the Hudson River at the former Fort Lee Dock, and enjoyed a lively tourist trade until this hotel was also destroyed by fire. Courtesy New Jersey Room, Fairleigh Dickinson University, Rutherford*

Sketch of the Palisades Mountain House, spectacularly situated on a precipitous cliff more than 300 feet above the Hudson River in what is now Englewood Cliffs. Guests arriving by steamboat were transported by carriages up a zig-zag macadamized route which would later be known as the Dykeman Street Ferry Road. The resort hotel could accommodate 500 people, and provided such amenities as hot and cold running water, with steam heat in the cooler weather. Erected in 1860, the Palisades Mountain House flourished until 1884 when it was destroyed by fire. From Art Journal, *n.s., v. 1 (1875)*

In 1887, the Scientific American *featured these plans for a "country dwelling" to be constructed in Rutherford. Notice the provision for flues for fireplaces or free-standing stoves in the parlor and in two of the bedrooms. Since no provision was made for a bathroom, the clients apparently opted for a portable bath tub. The instructions call for a "privy vault to be built where directed." Similiar homes in Rutherford were selling in the neighborhood of $3,000, with mortgages available beginning at $14 per month. Courtesy New Jersey Room, Fairleigh Dickinson University, Rutherford*

A DWELLING OF MODERATE COST AT RUTHERFORD, N. J.

The perspective drawing and plans shown on the colored plate presented with our present issue, and the accompanying sheet of details of construction form, with the specification below, a complete set as prepared by Mr. B. J. Schweitzer, architect, of No. 84 West Broadway, New York city, for the erection of a two story dwelling at Rutherford, N. J., for Mr. A. F. Garnier.

The design has been carefully considered with the view of providing a comfortable and convenient house at a moderate cost. The whole arrangement is a successful one in the cozy and snug appearance it presents and the attractive and appropriate elevation provided.

While keeping the cost strictly within moderate limits, the architect has employed only the best materials and construction, as will be apparent on reference to the specification.

The sheathing is of dressed hemlock boards, and is put on diagonally, and the roof is covered in with Bangor slates of a dark color, producing a very good effect.

Mr. Schweitzer has had a very extended experience in designing all descriptions of houses. In Rutherford, N. J., alone he is responsible for over a hundred buildings, while at Passaic and various other places on the Erie he is well represented by his characteristic work. His fifteen years' labor in New York and its vicinity has made him well known as a careful architect of originality and assiduity.

SPECIFICATION.

EXCAVATIONS.

Cellar.—To be under the whole house, 3 ft. 6 in. deep.

Cesspool.—To be 7 ft. in diameter and 8 ft deep, built where directed

Cistern.—To be 8 ft. in diameter and 10 ft. deep, built where directed.

Trenches.—For pipes to be at least 2 ft. 6 in. below the surface.

Piers.—All outside piers to be at least 2 ft. 6 in. below the surface. All inside piers 6 to 8 in. below the cellar bottom.

Privy Vault.—To be 4 ft. 6 in. long, 4 ft. 6 in. wide, and 4 ft deep, built where directed.

Grading.—Clean up the entire premises of all rubbish, and grade off earth around the house as directed.

MASON'S WORK.

Cellar Walls.—Up to the surface level, to be 18 in. thick, of Belleville quarry stone, laid in good lime and cement mortar. All to be bonded and pointed complete. Above the ground build a hard brick wall, 8 in. thick, laid flush with the inside of stone wall, in good lime and cement mortar. Point up complete.

Piers.—Build all piers of good, hard brick, laid in lime and cement mortar, and point up complete.

Chimneys.—Build chimneys as shown on plans, of good, hard bricks laid in lime and cement mortar; strike all joints on the inside and outside. Provide each room with a stovepipe hole, collar, and thimble, and cap them with a bluestone 1½ in. thick. Build the fireplace in kitchen for range, and furnish and set a bluestone hearth rubbed smooth, also a rubbed bluestone lintel, all complete. The jambs in the kitchen to be nicely pointed and laid up in select Hackensack brick.

Outside Cellar entrance to have bluestone copings and steps.

Cistern.—To be bricked up with good, hard brick, laid in cement mortar. An arch is to be sprung over the top, with a manhole and bluestone cover.

The inside is to be thoroughly cemented, and warranted water tight. The same is to have an overflow pit, and is to be connected with pipes from all leaders.

Cesspool.—To be stoned up dry in usual manner.

Privy Vault is to be stoned up dry in usual manner.

LATHING AND PLASTERING.

All walls and ceilings on first and second floors are to be lathed with spruce lath, and plastered two best coats of tempered mortar, and then hard finished hard and white.

CARPENTER'S WORK.

Timber.—All timber is to be of best quality hemlock. Corner posts, plates, and interties to be mortised and tenoned together, all 4" x 6".

All angles are to be braced with long braces.

First and second floor beams, 2" x 9", attic floor beams 2" x 8", all placed 16 inches from centers, and bridge all in a thorough manner, as directed.

Double all header and stringer beams.

All wall strips 2" x 4"; all openings to be studded with 3" x 4".

Rafters 2" x 8", placed 20" from centers.

Sheathing.—Cover the entire frames with dressed hemlock boards, put on diagonally, and put on resin sized sheathing paper over the hemlock boards.

Siding.—Cover the entire house, from sill to plate, as per drawing with No. 1 narrow lap siding.

Shingles.—Cover the gables and lean-to over the piazza with regular sawed round and square butt shingles of California redwood, laid 6 inches to the weather.

Trim Corner Boards, Window Casings, and Water Table, 1¼" best white pine. Main cornice all as per detail, of best white pine; also piazza trim, cornice, columns, and rails of best white pine.

Roofs.—All main roofs are to be covered with best Bangor slate in best manner. The ridges are to be coped with galvanized iron and made perfectly water tight.

Bay window and porch on rear are to be tinned with best I. C. tin.

All gutters are to be tinned with best I. C. tin, to conduct all water through 3" leaders.

Windows.—All sashes to be 1½" thick, glazed with double thick French sheet glass. The upper sashes are to have marginal lights filled with cathedral glass.

Furnish all with the "Ives" sash fastener, complete, and hang all sashes on cord weights and pulleys.

Blinds.—All windows to have outside blinds, hung in pairs, on New York wrought iron hinges, and all to be furnished with proper fastenings.

Doors.—Cellar doors to be of heavy spruce dressed, hung on hook hinges and furnished with lock. Front doors 1¾ in. thick, moulded as per drawing, hung on 4 in. by 4 in. hinges and furnished with 4¾ in. "Niles" patent lock and bronze furniture, all complete. Vestibule door to be glazed in upper part and to have marginal lights filled with cathedral glass; furnished same as front doors. All doors, except closet doors, 1½ in., four paneled, white pine, hung on 3½ x 3½ in. regular loose pin butts, and furnished with the "Niles" patent mortise locks, brass bolts and strikes. All closet doors 1¼ in. thick, hung on 3½ x 3½ regular loose pin butts, and furnished with "Niles" patent locks. All inside doors, except sliding doors, are to have jet knobs and electro-bronze roses, No. 47 E; sliding doors are to be hung on Prescott's brace hangers, and furnished with flush locks.

Floors.—All on inside are to be covered with ⅞ in. x 4½ in. merchantable white pine flooring. Piazza floors 1¼ in. white pine, laid with white lead in grooves. Piazza is to be ceiled in good and workmanlike manner.

INSIDE TRIM.

All window casings and door trim, 5 in. Queen Anne, with turned corner blocks; all good white pine. All windows to have aprons and stools. Base on first floor 1 in. x 9 in., on second floor 6 in., all good white pine.

Shelve all closets, and furnish all on second floor with hooks.

Stairs.—Newel on first floor, 7 in., turned cherry. Rail, 3½ x 4 in., double Queen Anne; balusters, 1¾ in., turned cherry; risers, ⅞ in.; treads, 1¼ in.; strings, 1¼ in.; all white pine. Attic stairs inclosed, built in a strong and substantial manner.

Cellar stairs built of dressed plank.

Sink.—Put in the kitchen an 18 x 30 in. sink, with drip board, all complete. Connect it with a 1¼ in. lead trap, back vented, and run waste to 2 inch cast water pipe, with fresh air vent and trap, before leaving the cellar.

Pump.—Furnish and set a No. 70 Douglas No. 2 pump, connect with 1¼ in suction to cistern, all complete.

Range and mantels will be furnished by the owner and set by the contractor.

Outhouse.—Build in usual manner.

PAINTING.

All metal to be painted two coats of metallic paint in linseed oil. All woodwork on outside painted two coats of white lead in linseed oil. Stain the inside and varnish two best coats of No. 2 varnish.

Finally, do all that is necessary to finish the entire house in a faithful and workmanlike manner, ready for immediate occupation.

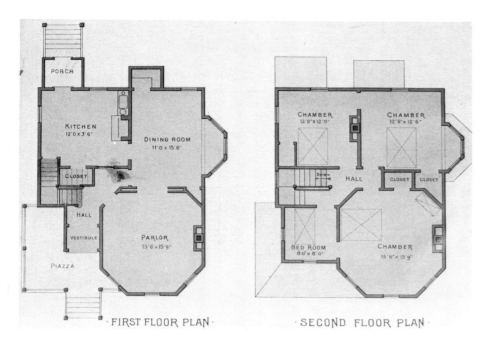

· FIRST FLOOR PLAN ·   SECOND FLOOR PLAN ·

Asymetrical massing of gables and turrets mark this picturesque Queen Anne style in the same neighborhood, still standing, although greatly altered, on the corner of Central and Summit avenues. Owned by F. Eugene Crassous, a New York broker, the property may be located on John G. Stead's 1900 auction map of Hackensack property (Chapt. 4), half way between the railroad station and the Hackensack Golf Club. Courtesy Johnson Free Public Library

J. H. Nield's house on Prospect Avenue in Hackensack was built Queen Anne style, easily identified by the use of a variety of surface materials including shingles and clapboards, and a profusion of decoration. The carriage house to the right of the picture sheltered the family's horse and carriage, perhaps more than one. In 1900 lots on Prospect Avenue sold in the neighborhood of $385 to $400. It was not unusual for a purchaser to buy three or four lots in a parcel. Courtesy Johnson Free Public Library

From its blocky proportions and low pitched roof, this home on Essex Street in Hackensack may be characterized as an example of the Italianate style, as reflected in round-head windows, tall first-story windows, and the classical details in the porch columns and window cornices. The Italiante style was frequently used in urban dwellings and commercial buildings during the mid and late nineteenth century.

Rutherford resident E. C. Hussey designed this residence for a fellow townsman, Henry C. Jackson, an early settler associated with the clothing trade in New York City. The building's style may be defined as High Victorian Eclectic, popular during the 1860s-1880s, which incorporated features from several architectural styles. Here Gothic Revival elements appear on the pointed arches of the windows, the gable trim, and steeply pitched roof. The plan was reproduced as Plate 31 in Hussey's Home Building, *published in 1876, in which the architect declared that "the design and proportions combine to produce a very pretty and pleasing effect." He would have been pleased to know his design has been adopted as the logo of the Historic Sites Survey of the Bergen County Office of Cultural Affairs. Courtesy Meadowlands Museum*

The Jackson house dining room was well-lighted with Tiffany-style dome, crystal table lamp and gas bracket beside the buffet. Decorative plates line the plate rail and the walls. A glass china closet displays crystal serving pieces. The high-backed chairs would have been of oak or walnut as was the rest of the furnishings. Courtesy Meadowlands Museum

Grigg's House was home to William Walter Phelps after his palatial mansion was destroyed by fire in 1888. The house stood on what is now the site of Holy Name Hospital, directly across Cedar Lane from the ruins of his former home. At the time of his death, Phelps, son of the first president of the Delaware Lackawanna Railroad, allegedly owned half of the present township of Teaneck. Pictured here is daughter Marion's room which reflects Victorian fondness for fussiness and clutter, and in this case perhaps, ball fringe. The lambrequin draping the mantle was a typical decorative element in the homes of the period. Courtesy Teaneck Public Library

In house decoration and furnishings Victorians were committed to the concept of plenty, and surrounded themselves with a variety of furniture and accessories, draped, whenever possible with fringed velour. Mantles, tables, cabinets and whatnots labored under a burden of pictures, lamps, ornaments and souvenirs accumulated perhaps over several generations. A draped easel occupies a place of honor in the parlor of this middle class home on Donaldson Avenue in Rutherford at the turn of the century. Courtesy Meadowlands Museum

The Blauvelt Mansion on Kinderkamack Road in Oradell was constructed as a summer home for Kimball C. Atwood, successful New York insurance executive. In 1926 the property was acquired by Hiram B. D. Blauvelt, from which family the estate acquired its popular name, "Bluefields," a literal translation from the Dutch. The picture shows the estate in 1900 before the porte cochere to the left of the main building was removed; and before Kinderkamack Road, that now busy artery, was paved in 1910. Courtesy Oradell Public Library

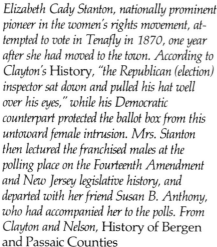

Elizabeth Cady Stanton, nationally prominent pioneer in the women's rights movement, attempted to vote in Tenafly in 1870, one year after she had moved to the town. According to Clayton's History, "the Republican (election) inspector sat down and pulled his hat well over his eyes," while his Democratic counterpart protected the ballot box from this untoward female intrusion. Mrs. Stanton then lectured the franchised males at the polling place on the Fourteenth Amendment and New Jersey legislative history, and departed with her friend Susan B. Anthony, who had accompanied her to the polls. From Clayton and Nelson, History of Bergen and Passaic Counties

Architectural historians have coined the term Chateauesque to describe the style popularized by Richard Morris Hunt who designed chateaux for the William K. Vanderbilts on Fifth Avenue and in North Carolina in the 1880s. In Rutherford, David B. Ivison, president of the American Book Company chose the style for "Iviswold," his summer home, designed in 1886 with towers resembling those of the Chateau de Chaumont, by William Henry Miller of Ithaca, New York.

Photographed here under construction, the brownstone building originally accommodated at least twenty-five rooms, splendidly furnished with wood work of walnut, mahogany and oak. The exterior was graced by a spacious veranda and two porte-cocheres, one of which has now been enclosed. Windows in the one remaining are inlaid with Tiffany glass.

The Ivisons summered in "The Castle," as it is popularly known in Rutherford, until David's death in 1903. During the 1920s it served as the clubhouse of the Union Club of Rutherford, which lost possession during the Depression. After a decade during which the building stood empty, it was acquired in 1942 by Fairleigh Dickinson Junior College, now Fairleigh Dickinson University. Courtesy Fairleigh Dickinson University, Rutherford

Not every man's house was a castle. Photo circa 1895 of the modest frame house which now stands, greatly altered, at 65 Godwin Avenue, Midland Park. Picket fence enclosures were a popular device used to protect lawns and gardens from illegally wandering cows, goats or other livestock. Gannon family traditions trace the building back to the 1830s. Pictured here are William Gannon's grandmother, his cousin, and his cousin's dog. Courtesy Midland Park Historical Society

No parade of the late 1800s would have been complete without a firemen's band. Here a Saddle River fire fighter relaxes after practice in the band room over the shoemaker's shop. His baritone, or alto horn was a favorite instrument in the brass bands of the late nineteenth and early twentieth centuries. Courtesy Saddle River Historical Committee

Katie Brown in front of the cottage she owned with her brother Tom one hundred yards north of Huyler Landing Dock on the slopes of the Palisades in the late 1800s. Karl B. Lamb photograph, courtesy Harold W. Tallman, Cresskill Borough Historian

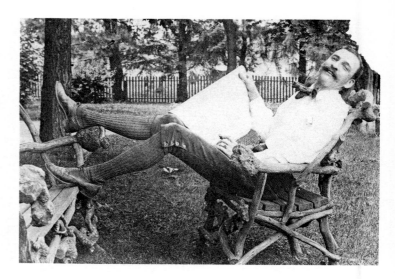

"What a joy it is to live in the suburbs! To awake mornings and to look out upon a broad sweep of sky; to throw one's window wide open, and to drink in an inexhaustible supply of fresh, clean, crisp air . . . ." L. A. Stout, pictured here enjoying country life in Ho-Ho-Kus would appear to agree with John Kendrick Bangs's appraisal. The prolific author's paen to suburban life was quoted in a promotional brochure issued by the Mahwah Company, land developers around the turn of the century. Courtesy Ridgewood Public Library

The Goetschius family pose in front of the frame house which may once have been a schoolhouse in the Saddle River area. On bitter winter nights the livestock were allowed to shelter in the cellar, entering through the door partly obscured by the horse. The well pump is barely visible in the left foreground, with what could very well have been the family privy just beyond. Indoor plumbing was by no means universal when this picture was taken circa 1895. Courtesy Home and Store News

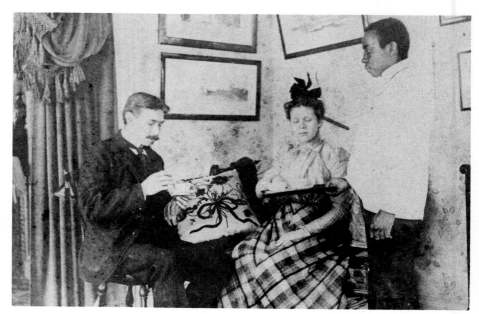

Harry Wilson takes tea with his sister Grace circa 1898 in the family home on Highland Cross in Rutherford. Grace Wilson was later married to John Ibsen Stousland, a sea captain who was a nephew of Henrik Ibsen, the Norwegian playwright. Courtesy Grace Schroeder, Rutherford

Although the family goat was probably more comfortable pulling the children's go-cart, the Huyler boys pictured here have harnessed him to a more prosaic task at their home in Tenafly. Courtesy Virginia Mosley, Tenafly Borough Historian

Lulu Doers of Park Ridge in the cycling costume popular with young women who took up the sport in the 1890s. Lulu's shirt is softened by a feminine cravat, but the cropped bell skirt, straw boater, high-buttoned shoes and black stockings were typical of the attire favored by fashionable feminine cyclists from Bergen County to Battersea Park in London. Courtesy Park Ridge Historical Society

As described in Van Valen's History of Bergen County, *Anton Molinari, first mayor of Wood-Ridge, was "Italian by blood, Polish by birth and American by adoption." A machinist by trade, in 1889 Molinari established a factory in Wood-Ridge which manufactured surgical instruments, the fore-runner of East Rutherford's highly successful Becton-Dickinson Company. From Van Valen,* History of Bergen County

David Quackenbush presented his card and his compliments when fulfilling social obligations in upper Bergen County at the turn of the century. Bearing many a familiar Bergen County name, these decorated calling cards were enclosed with gifts, invitations or announcements; left at funerals, or in the front hall card tray to announce a social call at a time when the family was not at home. *Collection of William Yeomans, Upper Saddle River*

In practice shoots prior to the Hackensack and Bergen Gun Club contest, high scorer, M. Halstead, was presented with an "elegant meerschaum segar holder." The Bergen County Democrat's report of the meet noted that "Artist" Vanderbeck's club photographs were "excellent specimins of photographic art." However, the news article neglected to supply the score. *Courtesy Bergen County Historical Society*

Private "field clubs" proliferated in Bergen County communities during the late 1800s. Organized by the athletically inclined, the associations provided facilities for a number of sports, and often fielded teams in organized games such as football and baseball, promoting town rivalries and spirited contests.

Baseball had been a favorite sport in Rutherford for more than a quarter-century before this picture was taken at the Rutherford Field Club's opening game on Memorial Day 1902. Chicken wire protected the spectators seated immediately behind home base in the grandstand which had been used during the previous decade by the Rutherford AC and the Wheelmen, probably the original owners. The stand shown here had been moved to Woodlawn and Delafield Avenues on the (then) outskirts of town, now the site of the borough's Tamblyn Field. Courtesy Meadowlands Museum

Rutherford Wheelmen, in assorted attire pose before the Dean residence still standing on Dean Court in Rutherford. Edward W. Dean, Jr., son of an early (1868) Ruther- fordian, stands seventh from left in the row of cyclists wearing traditional wheelmen attire. Organized March 21, 1885, Rutherford wheelmen were also active in baseball and track, and maintained an athletic field in Rutherford with a grandstand which could accommodate 300 persons. Courtesy Meadow- lands Museum

Civil War veterans of the Twenty-second Regiment Veterans Association celebrated their eighth annual reunion at the Hacken- sack Armory in late September 1896. The morning meeting was conducted by President Abraham G. Demarest, an officer of the regiment during the Civil War. At noon the veterans and their guests dined in the armory and reconvened at 2:00 P.M. for an after- noon of inspiring addresses and patriotic recitations. Following the ceremonies at the armory, the contingent marched through Hackensack, past houses and stores draped with flags and colorful bunting. Courtesy Special Collections, Alexander Library, Rutgers University

The Grand Army of the Republic was organized in 1866 to perpetuate the spirit of camaraderie experienced by Union soldiers in the camps and on the battlefields of the Civil War. The group was also influential in the establishment of Memorial Day as a national holiday, and G.A.R. members were conspicuous in the annual parades. The New Jersey Department was organized in 1867, but more than ten years passed before the first Bergen County post was instituted in Carlstadt in 1878. In 1881 the James B. McPherson Post appeared in Hackensack. Photographed here are aging members of the Gabriel R. Paul Post, No. 101, Westwood. The hatless man in the front row is William C. Herring, Bergen County sheriff from 1895-1897, and a past commander of the post. Courtesy Bergen County Historical Society

Those Rutherford businessmen who owned horses and vehicles were invited to participate in the Labor Day Parade of 1896, sponsored by the Butchers' and Grocerymen's Association of Rutherford. Spectators (or perhaps workmen) at right in the photograph, view the festivities from the Rutherford National Bank building under construction on Park Avenue at the foot of Sylvan Street. Courtesy Meadowlands Museum

July 13, 1895 proved to be a very unlucky day for the residents of Cherry Hill (now River Edge). A general storm spawned in the St. Lawrence Valley generated three separate tornadoes as it moved southward over New England, Long Island and Bergen County. Although the Cherry Hill tornado claimed only three lives, destruction in the area was widespread. Volunteers supplied tents and food for the homeless and solicited funds from the train loads of sightseers who arrived on the following day to view the devastation. Before the storm, Gil Jones's house stood on Hackensack Avenue in what was then Cherry Hill. Curious onlookers inspect the ruins of the Cherry Hill Hotel, where owner Conrad Friedman was killed by falling bricks from his walls and chimney. Courtesy Bergen County Historical Society

Portraits of Bergen County officers who served in the Second Regiment, New Jersey National Guard, during the Spanish-American War. Top row and center: regimental officers John Engle and Alfred T. Holley of Hackensack, Daniel A. Currie of Englewood. Bottom left, Addison Ely, captain of Rutherford's Company L; and at right, Frank S. De Ronde, captain of Company F of Englewood. The naval captain has been tentatively identified as John Jay Phelps, son of William Walter Phelps of Teaneck, who earned the sobriquet, "Captain," following his circum-navigation of the world in the yacht Brunhilde, following his graduation from Yale. During the Spanish-American War, however, John Jay Phelps held the rank of first lieutenant (acting) in the U.S. Naval Reserve. From Superintendent's Annual Circular of Greeting, 1900

Drummer boy of Rutherford's Company L is flanked by members of his company in their camp at Sea Girt, New Jersey. June 1898, their first post during the Spanish-American War. Courtesy Meadowlands Museum

Greeted by bells, whistles, and cheering throngs on both sides of the Hudson, and on every style of river craft, the North Atlantic Squadron steamed in review up the Hudson River on August 20, 1898, six weeks after their victory over the Spanish fleet in the harbor of Santiago de Cuba. Led by the armored cruiser, New York, seven battle ships in turn thundered twenty-one gun salutes at Grant's Tomb. This view was taken from Edgewater directly across the river. The spectacle lasted two and one-half hours, after which the squadron returned to its berth at Tompkinsville, Staten Island. Courtesy Edgewater Public Library

One could sit undisturbed on the old iron bridge in New Milford. Courtesy Johnson Free Public Library

As Bergen County entered the twentieth century, her leading citizens were rather pleased with the way of life that they enjoyed there. This satisfaction was no where more evident than in the descriptions evoked by J. M. Van Valen in his *History of Bergen County* published in that year. Consider, for example, his view of Hackensack in 1900:

Hackensack, as a place of residence, is unsurpassed by any other suburb of New York City. Beautifully situated on the west bank of the Hackensack River, from the commanding heights on its western border can be seen the river winding through the valley, with the range of the Palisades beyond and New York twelve miles in the distance. A population of 10,000 covers an area of 2,000 acres, thus affording wide streets, ample grounds and abundance of air and sunshine to the inhabitants.... The dwellings are chiefly built of wood, many of them surrounded by large lawns pleasantly shaded. There are no crowded tenement houses.

Clearly, Van Valen's image of Hackensack was colored by his recognition of what it wasn't. Many of the worst problems of the era had, fortunately, passed Bergen by. For example, there was none of the filth and overcrowding such as Jacob Riis had pointed to in his famous photographic study of Philadelphia, *How the Other Half Lives* (1890). Of course there were poor people in Bergen as there were everywhere, but they were not concentrated together in decaying urban neighborhoods as they were in New York, and in Newark and Paterson.

In seeking to put the best face on social patterns prevailing locally at the turn-of-the-century, Van Valen stressed the people's traditional sober and refined values. "The man who does not belong to a club," he wrote, "is the exception and not the rule." At the Union Club in Rutherford, for example, the object "is the social enjoyment of the members," through "stage entertainments, billiard, pool and bowling tournaments, informal dances, receptions, card parties, etc." Sale or use of intoxicating liquors was prohibited in the club, as was gambling of any kind. "These features," Van Valen concluded, "make it a desirable resort for all the members and a place where their wives or parents can find no objection to their attendance."

But looking back there were also signs in 1900 of the changes that were soon to overwhelm the older ways. In Englewood in the spring of 1900, for example, the mayor ordered the arrest of a local vendor for what seemed like an obvious offense, selling ice cream on a Sunday. When the jury found the defendant "not guilty," it contributed, in the words of one local historian, "to the joy of the liberal minded and the sorrow of those good citizens who walk in the narrow way." (*Book of Englewood*, p. 193). Those older, more narrow ways were in for more challenges as the twentieth century intruded itself into Bergen County.

For decades there had been talk about bridging the Hudson. In August 1900, for example, the *New York Herald* announced a proposal for construction of a double-decker bridge to cross the Hudson between Manhattan (just above Fifty-ninth Street) and West New York (just below the Bergen County line). Within a week a real estate developer's pamphlet was touting "Beautiful Edgewater Heights," just "15 minutes by trolley" from the future bridge site. Some of the trolley lines envisioned by the bridge developers did in fact exist. The first street railway in the area was built by the Bergen County Traction Company, incorporated in 1894. The first trolleys ran from the Edgewater ferry terminal up the Palisades to Leonia by 1896, after which extensions were constructed to Englewood and Hackensack. In Hackensack, Rutherford and other towns, grants of franchise agreements met resistance from those who objected to the unsightly tracks and wires and the intrusive noise of the clanging trolleys. Such local opposition made matters difficult for smaller companies and forced a pattern of consolidation which ultimately led to three or four companies controlling all of the business. Soon after the first line reached Hackensack in June 1900, operators were pushing out branches west to Paterson and Passaic and north as far as Suffern, New York. Several routes connected with Newark or Jersey City, but the most important destination was the Edgewater terminal where ferries embarked for 125th Street across the River.

The period from 1900 to 1920 saw the heyday of trolley transportation in Bergen County. The decision to develop most routes along public thoroughfares rather than private rights of way eventually caused trouble. Street traffic limited the speed of service the trolleys could provide. Moreover, in granting franchises, the municipali-

Gracious reminder of a more leisurely era, the Green in Hackensack is pictured here as it appeared around the turn of the century, together with its neighbors, the First Reformed Church and the Bergen County Courthouse (at right). A tiny remnant of John Berry's original grant, the small park served for centuries as the focus of village life. In colonial *times it harbored the whipping post and stocks; later the public gallows. The Continental soldiers who camped here in November 1776 were followed only a few days later by Hessian troops, a "horrid, frightful sight to the inhabitants," according to one eyewitness, as reported by John W. Barber, mid-nineteenth century historian. The foun-* *tain near the center of the picture commemorated the introduction of Hackensack's public water supply in 1874, and was presented with much fanfare by the Hackensack Water Company in behalf of Bacot and Ward, Jersey City contractors in their employ. Courtesy Johnson Free Public Library*

ties commonly required that the companies pay part of the cost of improving the streets over which their tracks were laid, thus literally paving the way for their competition. As automobiles and busses became common, the traction companies disappeared. By the late 1920s all but a few lines had ceased operations. Meanwhile the internal combustion engine began to leave its mark. Even before 1920 horse-drawn delivery wagons were gradually being replaced by motor trucks and family flivvers were appearing on the roads. Like the rest of America, Bergen was edging toward the motor age.

As the county's population swelled from 78,000 to 210,000 between 1900 and 1920, the growing numbers and increasingly varied types of people made it all but impossible for the social and cultural arbiters of the period to retain the veneer of Victorian propriety with which they had tried to control every dimension of late nineteenth century social life. The transformation of values was spurred on by the cultural entrepreneurs, the magazine and newspaper editors, the lecturers and artists and others involved in the commercialization of American culture. Frederick Law Olmstead's design for New York's Central Park, for example, represented a traditional concept which he called "democratic recreation." He sought to foster certain values in park visitors through restful enjoyment of the natural scenery, "an influence favorable to courtesy, self control, and temperence." The activities available in the park such as cycling, horseback riding and ice skating, demanded a level of individual skill and self-control. The

new amusement fads of the early twentieth century called more often for spectators (or consumers) than for skilled participants. Historian John Kasson has studied the development of Coney Island in the early 1900s to distinguish between the older ideal and the new popular culture form—the amusement park. Rather than being "uplifted" through the appreciation of nature, here people sought entertainment by "letting go" and submitting themselves to be manipulated and thrown about by machines. Bergen County's Palisades Park offers a striking example of this transition of values. In the 1890s the New Jersey and Hudson River Railway and Ferry Company advertised the "park on the palisades" much as Olmstead described Central Park, as "a beautiful natural" place. It comprised "about eighty acres of forest land" and had two picnic groves and an "athletic ground" which could be rented by Sunday schools or other organizations. They were proud that the park was "thoroughly policed and lighted" so that "ladies and children [would] find it especially attractive." It was clear that raucous or uncontrolled activities were unwelcome. By 1907 Palisades Park had begun to add amusement park attractions similar to many at Coney Island. The visitors who screeched in self-imposed fear as the ferris wheel carried them up over the cliffs or waited on line for their turn to be lurched about in another ride called the "figure eight" were seeking a different kind of excitement than their counterparts of a generation before. The original planners of the park had sought no more than to encourage people to ride the new

A quiet Sunday morning on State Street in Hackensack in 1904, disturbed only by the clip-clop of horses' hooves and the clatter of carriage wheels carrying churchgoers home from Christ Church. A bevy of young parishoners, clothed in their Sunday best, cluster near the church entrance, visible at center left. Other worshipers exit through the play of sunshine and shadow on the tree-lined street. Courtesy Johnson Free Public Library

trolleys to the end of the line. As tastes changed, the natural beauty of the area seemed to be an insufficient draw. Spectacles such as balloon ascensions and a wild west show were added to help attract a paying audience. Entrepreneurs such as the Schenk brothers who took over Palisades Park in 1910 and made it into a full fledged amusement park, were in business to provide their fun.

Bergen County's most obvious expression of the newly emerging mass culture was in the motion picture business. The earliest focal point for the American motion picture industry was at West Orange, a few miles to the south in adjoining Essex County, where Thomas A. Edison maintained his "invention factory." Before long, however, the dramatic scenery of the Palisades and the close proximity to the homes and haunts of the actors and actresses in New York City, brought dozens of productions out of the cramped studios which a score of companies had set up in lower Manhattan, into the Bergen County countryside. Then, between 1910 and 1920, many of the companies moved their permanent production facilities across the river. Movie companies such as the Champion Film Company, Eclair American Company, the Victor Film Company, Solax Company and World Pictures, most later to be absorbed into the larger studios, established headquarters in Fort Lee. Famous producers such as William Fox, Samuel Goldfish (later Goldwyn) and Jesse Lasky worked out of studio facilities here. In addition to providing an important element in the county's economy, the early motion picture studios contributed

dynamically to the newly developing forms of commercial mass entertainment. As people from Maine to California queued up at nickelodeon theaters and later at ornate movie palaces to see the latest "Perils of Pauline" or Charlie Chaplin comedy, they represented the development of an emerging national consciousness in which Bergen County had played a part.

The dawn of the new century brought with it a breath of political fresh air as well, a movement for reform known as Progressivism. Historians have suggested that there were at least two dimensions of this reform impulse, one on the national and state levels dealing primarily with political corruption and with inequities in an economy increasingly dominated by large corporations and trusts, and another on the local level directed toward more immediate social problems. The "New Idea," as the reform impulse was termed by New Jersey politicians, was largely a response to political favoritism and corruption. The state legislature, for example, had passed a series of rules and regulations that made New Jersey a haven for large business conglomerates and trusts. Local corruption was evident too as municipal officials found ways to profit personally from the sale of utility and transit franchises. Scandal struck home when charges were levelled against Bergen County officials for issuing corrupt contracts for construction of the new courthouse in Hackensack. A grand jury later cleared the men involved, but such charges could only increase public doubts about the reliability of their civic officials. Because Progressivism was

Proper Victorians in fashionable headgear (right) enjoy a picnic along Ho-Ho-Kus Brook in Ridgewood. Perhaps the gentleman on the rock caught a fish adding to the enjoyment of the afternoon. Courtesy Ridgewood Public Library

largely an urban based phenomenon, Bergen played a less active role than did more urbanized counties such as Essex, or Hudson. Perhaps the most respected spokesman of the movement from Bergen was Charles O'Connor Hennesey, elected in 1911 from his Haworth district to the state assembly. There he supported, among other progressive causes, the Seven Sisters Acts (which abolished much of the trusts' specially favored status) and the reform of the structure of county governments throughout the state. In 1912 he was the first choice of Governor Woodrow Wilson's reform Democrats to be Speaker of the Assembly, but the opposition blocked his election to that post.

The other dimension of Progressivism, the local efforts of citizens groups and individual reformers to address community social issues, was evident in Bergen too. Perhaps the best example of such a reform crusade had already reached its fulfillment as the new century began. Appalled at the destruction being wreaked on the beautiful Palisades, the New Jersey Federation of Women's Clubs lobbied the legislature to stop commercial interests from blasting the beautiful cliffs into trap rock and gravel

for road building and other construction. Led by such public spirited members as Miss Elizabeth Vermilye of Engelwood, they succeeded in 1900 in forcing the establishment of the Palisades Interstate Park Commission—an organization dedicated to the preservation of Bergen County's unique geological heritage. To some degree representatives of the old cultural elite used the reform spirit to seek local laws which would enforce patterns of behavior that had given way before more subtle forms of social pressure. Thus saloon licensing and Sunday blue laws became matters of sharp debate, issues which to a degree persist to this day.

National and state-wide reform efforts were stirred in part by the literary efforts of social minded writers who came to be known as "muckrakers." Upton Sinclair's muckraking classic *The Jungle*, for example, recounted hair-raising stories of everyday life among workers in the American meat packing industry and, with its graphic descriptions of what went into the sausage vats at some factories, led many a consumer to forswear their breakfast treats. In 1905 Sinclair devoted some of the royalties from this very successful book to establishing a cooperative

Private lawn parties provided sedate entertainment for many a languorous summer afternoon. The Baileys entertained on their attractive grounds on Kinderkamack Road in Oradell. The giant ginkgo tree at the left was purchased many years before by a previous owner from a sea captain who brought the plant as a curiosity from the Orient. Courtesy Oradell Public Library

living arrangement for fifty or more of his intellectual friends from New York in a former private school on the Palisades called Helicon Hall. Despite rumors of debauchery which upset the townspeople, Sinclair's experiment attracted such visitors as John Dewey, William James and young novelist Sinclair Lewis, at that time still a student at Yale. In 1907 a fire destroyed the place.

Another gathering of intellectual luminaries started in the summer of 1915 as a coterie of Greenwich Village artists and writers sought fellowship in a colony of frame cottages on the western slope of the Palisades at Grantwood. Dr. William Carlos Williams, local pediatrician of Rutherford and an already recognized poet, would drive over to visit his friends in Grantwood in his new Ford automobile. In decades to follow Williams would become the most celebrated of Bergen's literary figures. But there were others. Joyce Kilmer, who became poet of international fame, took his new bride to live in suburban Mahwah and joined the growing army of commuters as he travelled back and forth to his job at the *New York Times*.

As the period drew to a close, war clouds were gathering in Europe. World events hit home with a bang in 1917, when the munitions factory operated by the Canadian Car and Foundry Company in the Lyndhurst meadows blew sky high. Miraculously, no one was killed, but the monumental fire and the shells which continued exploding for several days thereafter, shocked the entire metropolitan area.

With the rest of America, Bergen County provided men and material for the successful prosecution of the war in Europe. One of those not to return was Joyce Kilmer. Bergen County housewives like their counterparts everywhere in America were asked to help preserve resources. The county's unique contribution to the war effort was occasioned by the construction of Camp Merrit which overlapped the boundaries of Creskill, Demarest and Dumont. Camp Merrit served as the main processing center for troops on their way to the European front. More than half a million men passed through during the camp's short history.

This postcard showed that summer was a time for lazy canoe rides on the Hackensack River. Courtesy Johnson Free Public Library

In the early 1900s, Bergen County still retained a number of farmsteads which contributed to a bucolic atmosphere. This view of a Wood-Ridge farm on Hackensack Street shows the property in 1911 when it was owned by Leopold Brandenburg. The farm stood on land originally purchased by George Brinckerhoff from Captain John Berry in 1685. During Brandenburg's tenure, the acreage was gradually reduced by land sales; the most extensive in the 1920s to the Sunshine City development, and later in 1942 to Wright Aeronautical Corporation. The farmhouse is shown here as it appeared before alterations which eliminated the gambrel roof. Note the hay barrack to the right and the large frame house in the distance. In 1954 the house was renovated and restored to serve as the Wood-Ridge Memorial Library. Courtesy History of Wood-Ridge Committee

Early in October 1903, heavy rains in the Passaic River watershed fell upon swollen tributaries and ground already saturated by an unusually wet summer and fall. From October 8 to October 11, almost twelve inches of water fell upon the Passaic River drainage area, triggering the most destructive flood ever recorded there. The river remained in flood until October 19, inundating Bergen County towns along its length from Elmwood Park (then Dundee Lake) to North Arlington. Wallington, pictured here, with the greater part of its residential section under water, was the most severely affected. Flood relief committees were immediately organized in the surrounding towns and soon wagon loads of food, furniture and clothing were on their way to the flooded town. Rutherford alone raised almost $2,000, including $81 donated by local members of the New York Stock Exchange. Other prominent contributors included William M. Johnson of Hackensack and J. Hill Browning of Tenafly. From: Report of the Passaic River Flood District Commission, *December 1, 1906*

A rocking chair ferry passenger rides the ingenious cable rig designed by Bis Westervelt of Oradell, when the stone bridge at the foot of Oradell Avenue was carried away during the Hackensack River flood of 1903. Photograph by William King. Courtesy Bergen County Historical Society

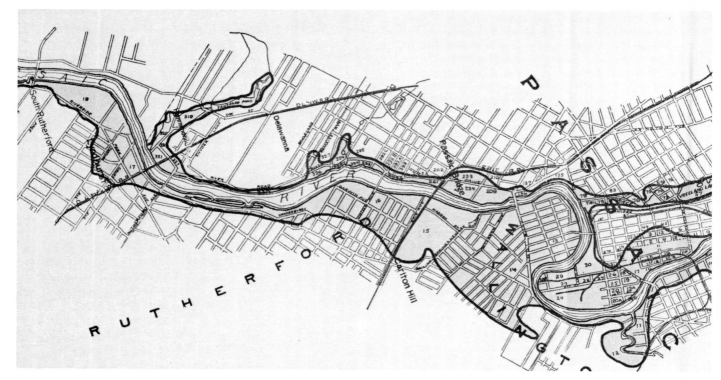

The heavy lines delineate the boundaries of Passaic River flood waters in 1903. Note the extent of the innundation in Wallington. From: Report of the Passaic River Flood District Commission, *December 1, 1906*

The Hackensack Water Company's pumping station at Oradell had more water than it could handle during the 1903 flood, with twenty-five inches in the engine room and several employees marooned in the plant by the water outside. This picture shows the works before the addition of a filtration plant completed the following year. Courtesy Oradell Public Library

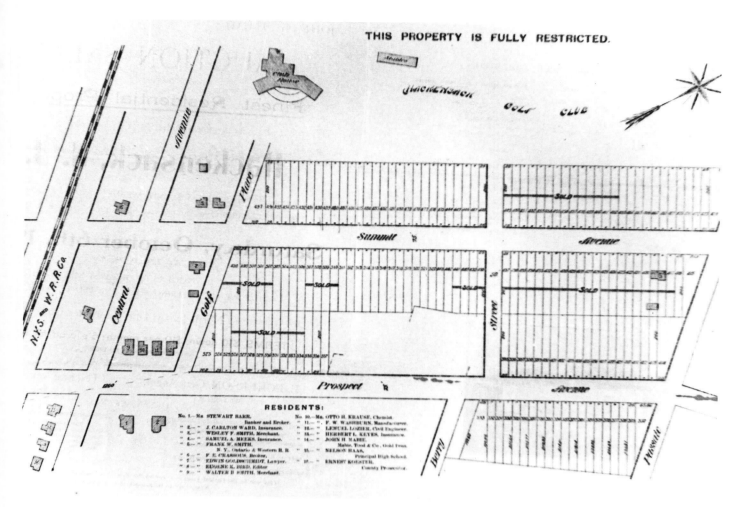

RESIDENTS:

No. 1.—Mr. STEWART BARR,
Banker and Broker.
" 2.— " J. CARLTON WARD, Insurance.
" 3.— " WESLEY F. SMITH, Merchant.
" 4.— " SAMUEL A. MEEKS, Insurance.
" 5.— " FRANK W. SMITH,
N. Y., Ontario & Western R. R.
" 6.— " F. E. CHASSOUR, Broker.
" 7.— " EDWIN GOLDSCHMIDT, Lawyer.
" 8.— " EUGENE K. BIRD, Editor.
" 9.— " WALTER B SMITH, Merchant.

No. 10.—Mr. OTTO H. KRAUSE, Chemist.
" 11.— " F. W. WASHBURN, Manufacturer.
" 12.— " LEMUEL LOZIER, Civil Engineer.
" 13.— " HERBERT L. KEYES, Insurance.
" 14.— " JOHN H. MABIE,
Mabie, Toad & Co., Gold Pens.
" 15.— " NELSON HAAS,
Principal High School.
" 16.— " ERNEST KOESTER,
County Prosecutor.

John G. Stead, Auctioneer.

AUCTION SALE

OF THE

Finest Residential Property

in the Most Exclusive Section of Progressive

Hackensack, N. J.

Magnificent PROSPECT and SUMMIT AVENUES, directly in front of the
Beautiful Golf Club Grounds, only 1200 feet to Prospect Ave. R. R. Station.

Saturday, October 6th, 1900,

AT 2.30 P. M.

THE GRAND SUCCESS OF OUR LAST SALE PROVES
THAT WE ARE OFFERING WHAT THE PEOPLE WANT.

Title Guaranteed by North Jersey Title Guarantee Co., Free of Cost.

TERMS, $10 down, $10 per month; 5 p. c. off for Cash.
No Interest or Taxes for 1900.

FOR MAPS AND FREE RAILROAD TICKETS APPLY TO

C. E. ECKERSON, Gen. Agent,   HACKENSACK LAND CO.,
183 Main Street,   116 Main Street,
HACKENSACK, N. J.

Maps and Tickets can also be obtained at
McBRIDE'S NEWS-STAND,
Arcade, 71 Broadway, N. Y.

GUSTAVE E. BEYER, Real Estate,
281 Sixth Ave., cor. 18th St., N. Y.

Train Leaves Penn. R. R. Depots:
West 23rd Street, - - 1.25 P. M.
Desbrosses Street, - - 1.30
Cortlandt Street, - - 1.30
Jersey City, - - 1.45
N. Y., Sus. & Western R. R.

This will be the Fastest Train ever ran on the New York, Susquehanna & Western R. R.—
Jersey City to Hackensack in seventeen minutes.

Real estate developers continued their aggressive promotions as evidenced by this 1900 brochure. The Hackensack Land Company aimed their promotion at the affluent commuter from New York City, and from the increasingly congested cities of Newark, Paterson and Jersey City. The map pictured here capitalized upon the property's proximity to the railroad station and to the Hackensack Golf Club, while the list of land-owners emphasizes professional men and white-collar occupations. Courtesy New Jersey Room, Fairleigh Dickinson University, Rutherford

Duplex or barrel car introduced by the Bergen County Traction Company in 1897 featured windows which could be rolled up under the roof during the summer. Courtesy Newark Public Library

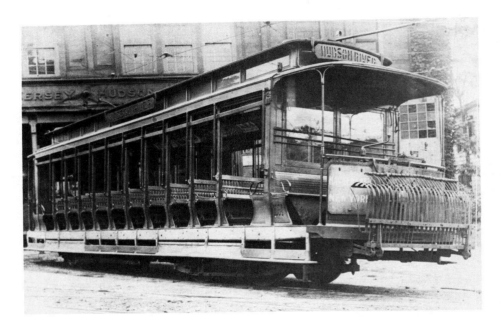

Open cars similar to the one pictured here were a summer feature of the trolley lines from their debut in 1900 until the introduction of one-man car operation circa 1926 rendered them obsolete. Wooden benches were arranged across the car with no provision for a center aisle. When the car was crowded, adventurous passengers sometimes rode the running boards much as they still do in San Francisco's cable cars. Courtesy Bergen County Historical Society

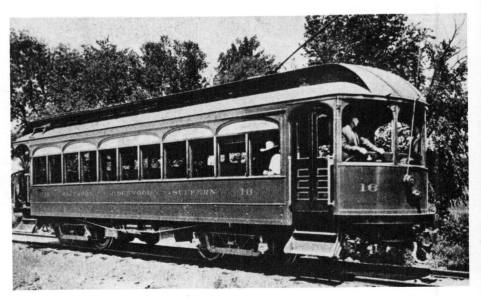

North Jersey Rapid Transit Company's Trolley shown here in a postcard view ran from East Paterson to Suffern through Ridgewood and Ho-Ho-Kus from 1912 until its abandonment in 1929. Courtesy Home & Store News

Passengers bound for St. Michael's Villa, a Catholic convent on the Palisades between Englewood Cliffs and Fort Lee, rode the trolleys of the Palisades Line. Opened for traffic in 1894, the line originally operated as a steam railroad, later changing to trolleys which ran from Coytesville to the West Shore Railroad ferries at Weehawken. This photograph was taken in 1912 at the Coytesville wye, the end of the line. Collection of the North Jersey Chapter, National Railway Historical Society

Trolley passengers rounding the landscaped horse-shoe curve cut into the Palisades above Edgewater in 1900 enjoyed an unparalleled view of the Hudson River from Yonkers to Staten Island. On a clear day one could see Long Island Sound. Although modern sky-scrapers interrupt the Long Island view, New York City lights and reflections on the river still provide evening spectaculars in the Borough of Edgewater just as they did almost a century ago. Postcard courtesy Johnson Free Public Library

In the southern section of the county, the Newark and Hackensack Traction Company connected those two cities in 1904 along a route similar to that of Public Service's 102 bus line (now route 76). This 1910 photo shows the motorman, and in the rear, the conductor who collected fares and signalled when it was safe for the trolley to proceed. The function of the lowered fender in front of the car was the same as that of the "cow-catchers" on early railroad engines. Trolley accidents were not uncommon, and the hapless pedestrian would be scooped up by the fender, away from the lethal trolley wheels. *Courtesy History of Wood-Ridge Committee*

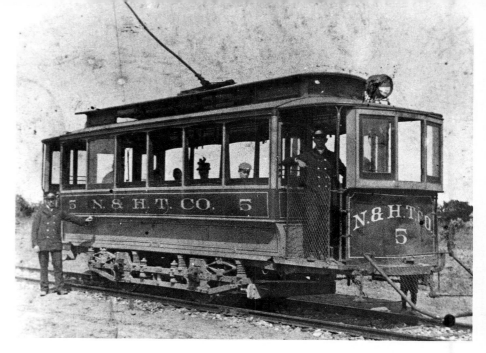

The automobile was also adopted with enthusiasm in Bergen County. In Ridgewood, Mr. and Mrs. Calvin Smith posed in their Maxwell runabout, "a favorite with the ladies," which was introduced in 1906 for $825. Mrs. Smith's veiled bonnet and enveloping coat, aptly termed a "duster," were designed to protect her clothes from dusty rides on unimproved roads. She holds protective goggles in her hand. *Courtesy* The Ridgewood NEWSpapers

Proud owners of the new vehicles soon discovered that driving the horseless carriages was not an unmitigated pleasure. Circa 1920, automobile accidents would have been curiosities attracting a number of interested spectators. This flivver met its fate on a summer evening on the corner of Cedar Lane and River Road in Teaneck. *Courtesy Virginia Mosley, Tenafly Borough Historian*

On Class Day at Park School in Rutherford, fortunate members of the Class of 1916 pose in that instant high school status symbol, the family Model T. Courtesy Meadowlands Museum

In another evolution of the transportation industry, the motor truck began to replace the horse and wagon. In 1908 Barney Smith hauled sweet corn, tomatoes, cabbage, spinach and potatoes by horse and wagon from his Glen Rock farm to Gansvoort Market on West Street, south of 23rd in New York City. In 1911 produce from the Smith farm was carried in a new motor truck, one of the first in the Glen Rock area. Courtesy Glen Rock Public Library

Retail stores also switched to the gas-powered delivery truck. Although horse power for J. Wiersma's Home Bakery was still the four-legged variety in 1913, not too many years later the Ridgewood Bakery was making deliveries by truck. In this photograph the driver is making a stop at the Ridgewood Country Club which appears in the background. The clubhouse was constructed in 1913 at a cost of more than $100,000. Club members enjoyed a "high-class cafe and restaurant, bowling alleys, billiard and pool tables and a fine dancing pavilion." Courtesy The Ridgewood NEWSpapers and Ridgewood Public Library

Years before the advent of gas or oil fuels, homes were heated by furnaces fired by anthracite or bituminous coal delivered in heavy, two-handled canvas bags which were stacked on a flat-bed truck such as the one above. Drivers hauled the coal to the proper basement window and dumped it down a metal chute to the coal bin below. Note that the Waldwick Coal and Lumber Company had a telephone connection for their customers' convenience. *Courtesy Paterson Museum*

The Fairmount Bottling Co. truck, manufactured by the Paterson Vehicle Company, was designed to transport liquids by the case. Compare this vehicle to the horse and wagon used by the Carlstadt Bottling Company at the turn of the century (chapter 3). *Courtesy Paterson Museum*

Julius Roehrs's handsome new delivery van was no doubt enclosed to protect the cut flowers and plants his firm had been supplying to the South Bergen area for more than thirty years. In 1892 Julius Roehrs maintained forty greenhouses along the Paterson Plank Road in East Rutherford. Eighteen of these were devoted to the growing of roses for which Mr. Roehrs won numerous prizes at the New York Flower Exhibitions. *Courtesy Paterson Museum*

Early competition to the trolley lines appeared in the decade before 1920. Here an inter-city bus stands before the Paterson Vehicle Company where it was manufactured in 1915. The open design and rolled curtains suggest the design of the horse-drawn surrey from which it undoubtedly evolved. In a later model, the body had been enclosed and the entrance moved forward to the driver's right. The Midland Park bus also offered its passengers protection from the weather. Entrance was apparently still from the rear. Note the chain-driven axel and the tire chains for traction on ice and snow. Courtesy Paterson Museum

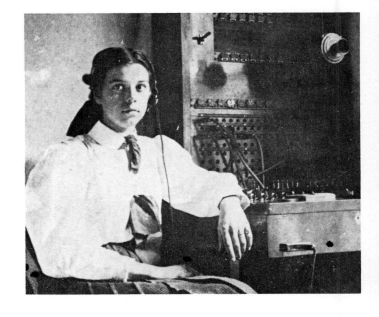

When Miss Helen Harvey first operated the local telephone exchange in Ramsey in the early 1900s, there were thirteen subscribers served by a fifteen-drop switchboard. Until its acquisition by New Jersey Bell in 1929, the exchange had been housed in drug stores and private homes, including Miss Harvey's home on Church Street. Courtesy Home and Store News

By 1920, telephone and electric wires were common sights in Bergen County "downtowns," and the automobile was no longer a rarity. Parking was evidently not a problem in Ridgewood on the summer day when a photographer captured this view of East Ridgewood Avenue from the corner of Prospect Street. Courtesy The Ridgewood NEWSpapers

During the summer, the wooded Palisades and the rural country beyond continued to attract city dwellers on both sides of the Hudson. In 1903 The Park on the Palisades was a picnic area promoted by the New Jersey and Hudson Railway and Ferry Company, successor to the Bergen Traction Company, to encourage traffic on its trolleys and ferries. Appropriately enough, the promotional calendar for the month of June featured the Hudson River shad. Courtesy Edgewater Public Library

Almost obscured by surrounding greenery, the park's refreshment pavilion offered "ice cream, light lunches and soda water" according to the promotional brochure. Courtesy New Jersey Historical Society

PALISADES
AMUSEMENT PARK
FORT LEE, N. J.

OPERATED BY THE AMUSEMENT SECURITIES CO.
A. H. DEXTER, PRESIDENT

A UNIQUE AMUSEMENT ENTERPRISE,
COMBINING THE BEAUTIES OF NATURE
WITH
HIGH CLASS, SELECTED AND REFINED
ATTRACTIONS AND AMUSEMENTS

Five years later the name had become Palisades Amusement Park, offering among other "high class amusements," a merry-go-round. From Dedication of Monument to Soldiers of the American Revolution, Fort Lee, New Jersey...1908. *Courtesy Bergen County Historical Society*

Balloon ascensions at the park also generated excitement and publicity, attracting enthusiastic fans. Courtesy Sol Abrams

Among other attractions, the Schenck brothers added a ferris wheel after they purchased the park in 1910. Daring riders experienced an extra thrill from their perch high over the Palisades as they viewed the sheer drop down the cliff to the river below. Courtesy Sol Abrams

"Doc" Willat's twin glass barns, one of the early Fort Lee film studios which were instrumental in creating a new American phenomenon, the movie star. Here Theda Bara lured countless men to their destruction under the cameras of Fox Films, adding a new term, vamp, to the lexicon of the emerging twentieth century. Willat's studios were also leased circa 1915-1916 by the Triangle Company, a Los Angeles-based firm whose movies starred such film personalities as Douglas Fairbanks and Fatty Arbuckle. Courtesy Fort Lee Public Library

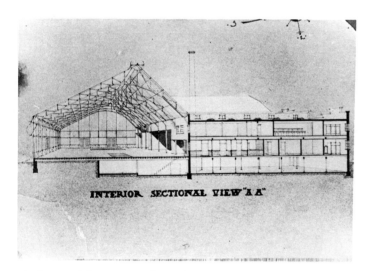

INTERIOR SECTIONAL VIEW "A A"

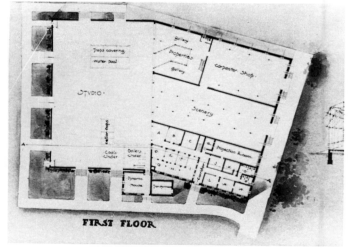

FIRST FLOOR

Architectural drawings for the Peerless Studios on Lewis Street in Fort Lee, built in 1914 by Jules Brulatour, owner of Peerless Pictures. Like the Willat, the Eclair and the Solax studios in Fort Lee, the buildings were designed for optimum use of natural light, and included dressing rooms, administrative offices, and photo lab, with areas for construction and storage of scenery. Courtesy Fort Lee Public Library

110

Interested on-lookers (foreground) on this Roman street on the back lot of Paragon Studios in 1917 undoubtedly included Fort Lee residents who were often hired as extras during the filming of such extravaganzas as Les Miserables or Orphans of the Storm. *Before the advent of talking pictures, background noise would have been no problem. Courtesy Fort Lee Public Library*

Pearl White photographed on an outcrop of the Palisades in a classic "cliff hanger" pose, movie jargon coined for her indomitable exploits, which also served to describe early serials which left their heros and heroines in desperate straits at the end of each episode. A veteran performer, Pearl White had appeared in films for four years before her most famous movie, The Perils of Pauline, brought her instant recognition and endeared her to contemporary movie audiences. This scene was from House of Hate, *a thriller filmed in 1918. Courtesy Fort Lee Public Library*

The early movies became so popular with the general public that Broadway producers were fearful that the new technology would supplant live performances on the New York stage. Pictured here is an early outlet for Fort Lee productions, the Pleasure Park Airdome, an outdoor theater which flourished in Wood-Ridge circa 1912. Harry Bringman of Wood-Ridge delivered films to Jantzen Brown, the operators of Pleasure Park, as an adjunct to his daily commute to New York City. *Courtesy History of Wood-Ridge Committee*

Hackensack's Windsor Debating Society poses before the Johnson Free Public Library circa 1912 for the photographer of the New York World. *Although no records of their debates have been uncovered, their preference in masculine headgear indicates that derbies have* it, two to one. Courtesy Hackensack Free Public Library

The tables are turned as members of the Paramus Valley Photographic Association get into the picture on one of the club's outings. Organized in 1903 to promote the "advancement of science and the art of photography," the association's 1905 exhibit featured thirty-three photographs of historic Bergen County houses, the work of Burton H. Albee, later president of the Bergen County Historical Society. Courtesy The Ridgewood NEWSpapers

William Carlos Williams, celebrated Rutherford poet, played third base for the Star Athletic Club. In this 1905 photograph Williams is kneeling at the right in the second row. His brother, Edgar Williams, the architect, appears at left in the row below. Courtesy Meadowlands Museum

In 1913 Wood-Ridge's bowling alley was a crude affair located in the former Wood-Ridge movie house; and heated, after a fashion, by a potbellied stove. Pins were set manually by local boys "whose dexterity in dodging flying pins," according to a local history, was beyond belief. The pin boy on the right may not have been quite so dextrous. A number of bowlers have removed their detachable collars, a masculine fashion which reduced laundry while promoting the sale of collar buttons. Courtesy History of Wood-Ridge Committee

113

In a timeless masculine rite still celebrated today, members of Ridgewood's White Star Athletic Club enjoy steak and beer in a patriotic setting, November 4, 1911. Courtesy The Ridgewood NEWSpapers

Feminine relatives of Oritani club members enjoyed all privileges except voting and holding office. Since they were not required to pay dues, a duty reserved for the family wage-earners, the women responded by raising revenue for club activities through fairs and bazaars. Their first fair was held in 1888 and raised $2,200. This photograph of "The Ladies' Committee" appeared in a supplement to the New York Sunday World, *circa 1912. Courtesy Johnson Public Library*

The Ridgewood Women's Club delegation posed for a picture before leaving for Atlantic City to attend the 1914 convention of the New Jersey State Federation of Women's Clubs. The Ridgewood club, organized in 1909, directed the activities of its membership toward civic and social reform. Courtesy The Ridgewood NEWSpapers

Two masculine pale-faces appear to have infiltrated the Degree Team, Minehaha Council, Daughters of Pocahontas in Hackensack. Courtesy Johnson Free Public Library, Hackensack

The Red Men's float in Ramsey's Firemen's Parade, July 4, 1912. Certainly one of the most colorful of the nation's fraternal organizations, the Improved Order of Red Men was represented by nine "Tribes" in Bergen County. A secret society with rituals known only to the initiated, members of the Red Men received benefits during long illness, funeral benefits, and some protection for widows and orphans. Courtesy Home and Store News

The elementary school provided an important step in the acculturation of the immigrant family as their children were introduced to the language, customs and traditions of American life. These eighth-grade graduates attended Market Street School in Dundee Lake, now Elmwood Park, on the Passaic River opposite Paterson's busy mills. In 1911 the class included a Talosia, a Gorchi, and a Sudek. Courtesy Elmwood Park Public Library

Members of the Bohemian Club enjoy an outing at the Velehradsky homestead in Dundee Lake, now Elmwood Park, circa 1900. Before being renovated into one large and several smaller apartments, the building was known as the Race Track Hotel. The porch at the right leads into the hotel's dance hall. Route 80 now passes directly over the site. Courtesy Elmwood Park Historical Society

Elementary school buildings in the early twentieth century were invariably square or rectangular boxes dominated by classrooms with little provision for specialized areas such as gymnasiums. Here Rutherford elementary school children perform calisthenics for the photographer, an exercise period which, if memory serves, was always the occasion for wide-open windows, no matter what the weather. Note the formality of the classroom with its rigid rows of desks, often nailed firmly to the floor. The spotless blackboards were no doubt neatly erased for the occasion. Circa 1912, the classroom was still lighted by gas. Courtesy Rutherford Public Library

Rutherford schoolchildren greet the springtime with their maypole, a custom borrowed from medieval England which was apparently popular in the elementary schools. During the maypole dance, children holding ribbons would weave in and out of the circle until their patterns produced a thick and colorful plait around the center pole. *Courtesy Rutherford Public Library*

One year after the opening of the J. Hull Browning Elementary School in Tenafly, the girls' basketball team posed in high shoes and hair bows for a team picture. Thanks to the foresight and financial aid of John Hull Browning, president of the Tenafly Board of Education, these young ladies would have had access to classes in drawing, sewing and cooking; courses not generally offered at the elementary level in the early 1900s. Browning, for whom the school was named, was a merchant and financier who was also president of the Northern Railroad of New Jersey. Now known as Browning House, the school building has been converted into condominiums. *Courtesy Virginia Mosley, Tenafly Borough Historian*

Fire companies continued to enliven parades on public holidays and other celebrations. Here small boys escort the Wood-Ridge hose cart as it proceeds along a street in the town of Wood-Ridge, circa 1912. The smaller hose cart behind the banner may well have been Wood-Ridge's first piece of fire-equipment, a hand-drawn hose reel pulled by three firemen while other firemen ran alongside on their way to the fire. *Courtesy History of Wood-Ridge Committee*

Tenafly's Police Department was formally established by ordinance in 1918. Chief George McLaughlin seated left in the first row, had kept the peace in Tenafly from his appointment in 1894 at a salary of $35 per month. *Courtesy Virginia Mosley, Tenafly Borough Historian*

Flag-waving Edgewater children in a model of civic participation, follow the colors down Hilliard Avenue to take part in the ceremonies at the laying of the cornerstone at Municipal Hall in 1904. Courtesy Edgewater Public Library

Ridgewood's mobile patrolmen and their bicycles circa 1916. An outgrowth of the Village Protective Association formed in the early 1890s, at the time of this picture, Ridgewood's police force included a super-intendent of police, one sergeant, seven patrolmen, a clerk and a German shepherd. Courtesy The Ridgewood NEWSpapers

Designed in the classic style, the Bergen County Courthouse, erected 1912, has been called one of the most imposing public buildings in New Jersey. Courtesy Newark Public Library

Hackensack, N.J., June 30th 1910

Mr. George Foster

The corner stone of the new County Court House will be laid with appropriate ceremony on Wednesday, July 6th, 1910 at 3 P. M. and you are cordially invited by the Committee to grace the occasion with your presence

James M. Galnac
George M. Brewster
Walter Christie
Committee

Mr. George Foster was an honored guest at the ceremonies attendant upon laying the cornerstone of the new county courthouse in Hackensack. Courtesy Bergen County Historical Society

RAMSEY BOROUGH REPUBLICAN CLUB

WILLIAM H. TAFT.

JAMES S. SHERMAN.

THOMAS FOXHALL   FOR MAYOR JOHN B. FINCH

This elaborate banner was erected by the Ramsey Republican Club in front of the Bergen Hotel on Main Street during the election of 1908. Courtesy Home and Store News

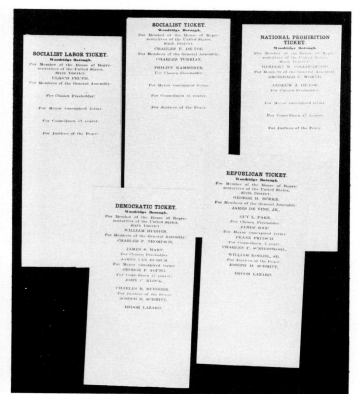

According to John Y. Dater, Ramsey historian and founder of the Ramsey Journal, *election tickets such as these were considered official ballots when certified by the county clerk. Candidates for election would substitute "pasters" bearing their own names which would be pasted over the printed names of their opponents. After a supporter dropped the altered ticket into the ballot box, he would then return to the candidate the ticket he had originally received from the clerk at the polls. On occasion, the resulting hand-shake might include a one or two-dollar bill. These election tickets from Wood-Ridge were prepared for the election of 1906. Courtesy* History of Wood-Ridge Committee

Members of Hasbrouck Height's Home Defense Company surrounded the unit's Gatling gun, a type of machine gun introduced during the Spanish-American War. Armed with 125 Springfield rifles and 75 shotguns, the company drilled twice weekly at Lemmerman Field and used the Hasbrouck Heights Field Club as an armory. Although two hundred recruits responded to the call of the borough's Preparedness Committee in April 1917, the company later dwindled to seventy-five. In 1918 the unit became part of the State Militia Reserve. Courtesy Hasbrouck Heights Public Library

Marching with fixed bayonets in military precision, Ramsey's Home Guard added a note of reassurance to that town's Fourth of July parade in 1918. Courtesy Home and Store News

Uncle Sam and Miss Liberty lead Ramsey schoolchildren in a patriotic show of solidarity on July 4, 1918. Courtesy Home and Store News

A branch of the Hackensack chapter of the American Red Cross, the Hasbrouck Heights Red Cross was organized in February 1917. From the original membership of twenty-two women, the chapter grew to more than seven hundred during the following year. During that time the membership raised over twelve thousand dollars and produced more than sixty thousand pieces of surgical dressings, hospital and refugee garments. Four tons of clothing were gathered for northern France and Belgium, and four hundred jars of jelly were sent to Camp Merritt Hospital. Courtesy Hasbrouck Heights Public Library

A typical fund-raiser, Ridgewood's Red Cross "Victory Bazaar" was held in the Garber Square area just west of the Erie Railroad tracks on July 4, 1918. The photographer unfortunately failed to highlight the Italian booth, shaped like a gondola and attended by four "real" street musicians playing mandolins and guitars. Three officers from the Italian Mission to Washington also graced the booth which vended goods made only in Italy. Courtesy The Ridgewood NEWSpapers

This 7,000 ton steel cargo ship was named Tenafly *in recognition of that borough's outstanding contributions to war-time Liberty Loan drives. Nancy Mary Sisson of Tenafly was photographed at Shooters Island where she christened the* Tenafly *at its launching on November 16, 1919. Courtesy Virginia Mosley, Tenafly Borough Historian*

Edith Buck in white at left center in the doorway of the Y.M.C.A. "hut" in France. The soldiers hold poppies, immortalized by British officer John McCrae's poem, "In Flanders Fields," as the symbol of the soldier's sacrifice for his country. Courtesy Ridgewood Public Library

Edith Sherman Buck of Ridgewood was one of a number of Bergen County women who volunteered their services in behalf of the American "doughboy." Her formal portrait taken in Paris in 1919 is shown here. Courtesy Ridgewood Public Library

From November 1917 to November 1918, more than half a million men marched through the country towns of Cresskill and Dumont between midnight and dawn, on their way from Camp Merritt to trains or to river ferries at Alpine which would take them to Hoboken, their port of embarkation. Begun in 1917, Camp Merritt finally occupied 770 acres in Cresskill, Dumont, Demarest and Haworth, with 1314 buildings in an area one mile long and three-quarters of a mile wide on either side of Knickerbocker Road. The nation's largest embarkation camp, its daily population fluctuated from twenty-five thousand to thirty-five thousand men, the majority of whom stayed only three or four days on their way to or from, the European theatre of World War I. In this candid shot, transient soldiers relax on beds airing in a company street, Camp Merritt. Courtesy Special Collections, Alexander Library, Rutgers University

Black soldiers pose at Camp Merritt on their way home from France. Courtesy Special Collections, Alexander Library, Rutgers University

The echo of tramping feet has long since died away, and Camp Merritt's temporary structures no longer exist, many of them destroyed in a fire so spectacular that fire companies from as far away as New York City were dispatched to put out the blaze. The Camp Merritt Monument alone remains as a reminder of the more than one million men who passed through Bergen County on their way to and from the first World War. Located within a small traffic circle at the intersection of Madison Avenue and Knickerbocker Road in Cresskill, the monument stands at what was formerly the center of Camp Merritt. At dedication exercises on Memorial Day 1924, General John J. Pershing and New Jersey's governor George S. Silzer addressed a crowd of several thousand. Courtesy Harold B. Tallman, Cresskill Borough Historian

chapter 5

Organized in 1917 as a one-man operation, the Bergen County Police Department was enlarged and motorized in 1921 to patrol county roads in an effort to relieve local law enforcement officers unable to cope with the numerous accidents and traffic violations which accompanied the increase in motor transportation. Early members of the county police are pictured here with their motorcycles at the department's original headquarters on West Mercer Street in Hackensack. Courtesy Bergen County Police Department

More Growing Pains

The years after 1920 were dramatically marked by the country's love affair with the automobile. Transformed, by the way of Henry Ford's assembly lines, from a rich man's toy to a working man's dream, no other product of mechanized production proved as pervasive an influence on the American life style in the years following World War I. The journey to work, housing development, shopping habits, summer vacations—these were but a few of the social and economic patterns which would be forever changed. Hitching posts and feed stores became anachronisms as gas stations, highway billboards, and eventually shopping centers sprang up on the land. No place in America felt this influence of the automobile more than Bergen County.

Whether or not the automobile made life better, it certainly made it more complicated. Dirt or gravel roads, for example, had proven serviceable for centuries; even when they were deep with snow or swamped with rain, horses could muddle through. Main streets in most New Jersey towns remained unpaved through the beginning of the twentieth century. Cars presented new problems, however. To achieve the speed that they were capable of, drivers demanded that roads be paved and even. In winter the snow had to be scraped away if cars were to find traction. Municipal budgets strained to meet the demands of motorists for better streets. Since before World War I Bergen County had shared the nation's passion for improving and widening existing roads and constructing new highways. Through the absorption of key thoroughfares previously maintained by municipalities and through extensive construction projects, the county road system expanded from 179 miles in 1920 to 342 in 1930 and nearly 500 by 1939. During the same period the state highway department developed 78 miles of highways in Bergen County as part of a state-wide plan adopted in 1926.

The obvious focal point of Bergen County road development in the 1920s and 1930s was the George Washington Bridge, the fulfillment of decades of planning. The concept of a Hudson River crossing had been addressed by the legislatures of New York and New Jersey as early as 1834. Technological progress marked by the dramatic opening of Roebling's Brooklyn Bridge in 1883, Bergen County's 200th anniversary, focused the continuing debate on whether the crossing should be a tunnel or a bridge. By 1910 there were two railroad tunnels under the Hudson, but a vehicular tunnel was not available until the one named for its builder Jerome Holland opened in 1927. Northern Bergen commuters remained dependent upon the ferries, and long lines of automobiles waited daily at the ferry slips.

The Port of New York Authority (Now the Port Authority of New York and New Jersey) had been created in 1921 by New York and New Jersey to develop and coordinate transportation in the region. Almost from its inception the authority aggressively persued plans and funding for the proposed bridge. Work on construction eventually began in the spring of 1927 according to the designs drawn by the famed architect Cass Gilbert and bridge engineer O. H. Ammann, and ground was broken on the Fort Lee side that September. Over the next four years two huge towers (twice the height of the Palisades) were erected and strung with cables (almost four feet in diameter) from which the concrete roadway was suspended 250 feet above the water. Eventually the decision was made to alter the original design, foregoing the granite facing that was supposed to be placed over the steel framework of the towers and leaving the massive and beautiful superstructure open to view. On October 24, 1931, fifty-nine million dollars and fourteen worker's lives later, the ceremonial ribbon was cut by New Jersey governor Morgan F. Larson and then New York governor Franklin Delano Roosevelt. In the majestic George Washington Bridge, at the time the longest suspension bridge in the world, Bergen gained a landmark second only to the Palisades themselves, and recognized everywhere. For a people depressed and unsure of their future the bridge, like the Empire State Building and Hoover Dam, stood as a monument to the promise that technology held out if it only could be harnessed to the service of man.

The new bridge and highway network created a dramatic impetus to Bergen County suburban development. Actually, the mere promise of the bridge was enough to provide a field day for real estate promoters. As early as 1922 the vast Teaneck estate of William Walter Phelps was opened for development. That community boomed for the rest of the decade, increasing its population 300 percent during the 1920s. In 1926 alone 471 new homes sprouted from the Teaneck countryside. Models were on display at West Englewood Manor in Teaneck, a development which emphasized the "authorized Hudson

Wider ownership of the automobile was followed by a corresponding increase in paved roads and streets, but improvements came slowly in the rural areas. Here a lone automobile negotiates a winding country road in Upper Saddle River in 1924. Courtesy Newark Public Library

A ride along the winding descent of the Palisades from Englewood Cliffs to the Henry Hudson Drive below provides a spectacular introduction to the scenic highway cut into the face of the Palisades. Opened for public use in October 1921, the five mile highway is maintained by the Palisades Interstate Park Commission. From Edgewater to Alpine, the Henry Hudson Drive provides unparalleled views of the Palisades cliffs and the river to the east. Courtesy New Jersey Historical Society

River bridge" in its promotional literature. In Wood-Ridge, developer Charles Reis was beginning his experiments in mass produced housing with 800 units on a 100 acre tract which he called "Sunshine City." In some ways the real estate boom in Bergen in the late 1920s resembled what was going on in Florida and southern California at the time. As one Bergen County realtor remembered: "our agency worked night and day." According to another, "vacant lots and acreage of all types found a ready market." In the excitement speculators puffed up land values to levels that made forclosures inevitable in the depression decade to come.

Perhaps the most ambitious development plan was the one put forth by New York City apartment house tycoon Charles Paterno. Having built successful high rise apartment houses on Park Avenue, West End Avenue, and Riverside Drive, now with the bridge approved, Paterno proposed to extend his enterprise across the Hudson with a six-building high-rise "apartment house city," a "Riverside Drive on the Palisades" for Englewood Cliffs and Tenafly. Though plans were published as early as July 1925, the town fathers of both communities hemmed and hawed for several years, delaying approval because of the increased pressure such a development would bring to bear on municipal services. Paterno's plans were eventually foiled by the financial contraction following the stock market crash of 1929. In the words of one local historian, however, "it was an ill wind which blew Englewood Cliffs some good." By the time extensive high rise development did begin in earnest, zoning regulations had been developed to preserve at least to some extent the suburban nature of these communities.

One outstanding Bergen County development, significant especially for its audacious design, was Radburn, then as now a part of Fair Lawn. Opened to home buyers and tenants in 1929, Radburn's plan incorporated some of the most innovative design concepts of the day. In Radburn, single family houses and apartment house units opened onto a "continuous strip park," and traffic was kept separate from other activities by arching overpasses. Two suburban "superblocks" were laid out with houses facing the park land and pedestrian walkways, with a park setting for the school which was to double as community and cultural center, and with pre-planned shopping facilities nearby. Cars were parked on cul-de-sacs at the rear of each unit thereby providing a safer, cleaner and more pleasant atmosphere for living. Although hopes for

expansion of the original two superblocks were dashed by the depression, the concept was borrowed and built upon by other innovative communities in Europe, Canada and the Soviet Union. Now, more than a half-century old, Radburn is still a self-contained community. There are new problems, such as finding space for parking the two or three cars common in today's households, but residents continue to enjoy Radburn's uniquely planned suburban atmosphere.

The short burst of real estate development occasioned by the bridge was cut short by the Depression of the 1930s. Bergen County's suburban potential was destined by circumstance to be held in abeyance until after World War II. Other areas of the economy, however, continued to react to the increased popularity of the automobile. By the late 1920s trolley lines were being rapidly replaced by busses, and more people were relying upon their cars to get them to work. The railroads were safe for the moment, but the internal combustion engine was reshaping the way people looked at their communities and themselves.

As the early advertising brochures repeatedly emphasized, suburban developments had always been built along the railroad. People lived within walking distance of the station, and it was therefore possible for communities to retain some of the cohesiveness of a traditional neighborhood in which people knew and cared about one another. In addition, as Daniel Boorstin explains, the "rails of street cars, like those of the steam railroads, tended to keep the city in focus." The trains and trolleys "brought customers to department stores, visitors to museums, and audiences to theaters, and so built downtown." In Hackensack, the trolleys and trains brought customers for the downtown stores and movie theaters like the ornate and beautiful Oritani.

Widespread use of the automobile in the 1920s and 1930s had freed the individual from the confines of the rails. Cars and busses could go anywhere and the consequent social and economic mobility was destined to change forever Bergen County's former patterns of commercial life. To survive, neighboring grocery stores found it necessary to compete with new marketing chains by advertising prices, installing refrigeration equipment, and redesigning for self-service operation. At least a few wives and mothers had already begun to think of themselves as chauffeurs as well as homemakers. In their recent history of Mahwah, Henry Bischoff and Mitchell Kahn quote a

Commuters debark at Edgewater from ferries arriving from New York City. The waiting trolleys are bound for Paterson, Hackensack, Fort Lee, Englewood and other towns behind the Palisades. Courtesy Public Service Electric and Gas Co.

1924 issue of the *Ramsey Journal* which published a poem entitled the "Mahwah Chaufferette." The poet was a local mother who assumed the logical penname "Mahmere." At about the same time a local minister preached a sermon entitled: "If Christ Came to Mahwah, Would He Be a Commuter?" The planners of Radburn had been sensitive to the changes wrought by the automobile and had tried to limit its impact. Before long, to paraphrase Lewis Mumford, "instead of buildings set in a park," Bergen County would have "buildings set in a parking lot."

In a larger sense, the automobile was but one example of the participation of Bergen County in the growing mass consumption economy of twentieth-century America. Through subtle suggestion or through bold and direct advertising, movies and radio, newspapers and magazines led people to seek satisfaction and meaning in their lives through accumulation of the symbols of material prosperity. The private home and the automobile were both obvious status indicators, but so were work-saving household appliances such as the electric refrigerator which allowed people to shop once a week at the supermarket (Bergen's first was Parker's which opened in Hackensack in 1935) rather than stopping more frequently at the neighborhood grocery. Another convenience introduced in Bergen County in the mid 1920s was the household oil burner. Not only was it cleaner than the old coal furnace, it provided even heat, thermostatically controlled, and was, like almost everything else, available on the installment plan. Perhaps most importantly, as noted again and again in advertisements in such magazines as *Charm*, published for New Jersey homemakers by Bamberger's department store in the 1920s and early

1930s, our lives could be free forever from the "shadow of the coal shovel."

The rich were getting richer during the 1920s, but the differences between the classes could be seen as more quantitative than qualitative. The new mass culture seemed to be a more democratic one. Music, comedy and drama, the finest entertainment the nation had to offer, was within the reach of everyone. This inevitably increased the pressure upon local cultural forms. The monthly recitals of the Semper Fidelis Orchestra at the Presbyterian Church in Wood-Ridge, for example, had to compete with "Amos and Andy" and "Fibber Magee and Molly" for their audience. The homes and cars of the wealthy were elegant and impressive, but the family Model T got there just the same, and almost any department store clerk could save up enough to drive away to the mountains or the seashore for a special weekend.

The mass media had helped to create the fascination for the airplane that swept across America in the 1920s. Tiny Teterboro, Bergen County's smallest municipality, became the focus of national attention as its airfield played host to daredevil airshows and to such famous fliers as Amelia Earhart, Charles Lindbergh and Admiral Byrd. Teterboro also boasted one of the country's most prominent early aircraft manufacturers. Anthony Fokker, the young Dutchman who founded the company, had made his first million before he came to America, by inventing the synchronized machine gun that made it possible to shoot through a revolving propeller. In the 1920s, Teterboro-built Fokker tri-motors spanned the Atlantic and Pacific on historic flights which captured the imagination of all America and paved the way for commercial aviation

in the United States. By 1932 Fokker returned to Holland in the wake of bad publicity following the crash of one of his planes in which famed football coach Knute Rockne had lost his life. Several years earlier Fokker had sold his factory to General Motors which now moved the operation to Virginia leaving behind two hangars and a few private planes. The abandoned Fokker factory buildings were transformed first into a marathon dance hall and later into a boxing arena. In 1937, the establishment of Bendix Aviation Corporation there started a new era in Bergen's aviation history.

All sorts of other fads and fashions found their expression in Bergen County during this time. In the summer of 1930, for example, two crazes swept through local communities. Miniature golf (or "toy golf" as it was called) was being played everywhere that summer, causing annoyance for people who lived nearby. Opponents of one "toy golf club" proposed for Rutherford feared that the private association would instead become a speakeasy, despite the assurances of the organizers that besides golf they planned nothing more exciting than a few minor concerts or an "afternoon tea." Meanwhile in Hackensack, a bicycle endurance marathon was testing the mettle of the local youth. A flat tire and a broken bike chain ended the efforts of the Hackensack team at just eight minutes short of sixteen days, but other teams droned on in neighboring towns such as Harrison, Kearny and Newark.

The period had its seamier side as well, of course. Prohibition brought illegal stills, speakeasies and a general spirit of lawlessness to Bergen as it did to the rest of America. News reports of police raids on bootleggers and "disorderly houses" became common. In 1932 an explosion

drew attention to a still being operated in the Meyerhoff brick factory. Local chapters of the Women's Christian Temperance Union continued to argue their cause. But the Bergen County division of the Women's Organization for National Prohibition Reform recommended repeal as a solution to the seeming epidemic of crime and corruption. All of Bergen's 12 delegates to the state's special ratification convention in 1932 voted to end prohibition.

An even more unpleasant blot on the memory of the period was the Ku Klux Klan. The post Civil War terrorist organization had been resurrected in the South in 1915 and by the mid 1920s had four to five million devotees across America. New Jersey was a center for activities in the Northeast, and Bergen County had more than its share of hooded klansman parades and cross burnings. Intimidation was their most vicious weapon. In 1923 a Lutheran minister in Ridgefield Park was warned by the Klan to get out of town. A few months later a real estate agent in Closter found his office painted red and a KKK emblazoned on his door. *The New York Times* reported later that year that Bergen and Hudson County klansmen had withdrawn support from the national organization because of a dispute over leaders and membership fees, but traditional Klan activities went on as usual. In 1924 a Roman Catholic seminary was terrorized by bomb blasts and burning crosses and in 1925 hooded brothers paraded in North Hackensack. The Klan fever seemed to peak in 1927 when an estimated 5,000 klansmen from Bergen, Hudson, Passaic and Essex counties rallied in Wood-Ridge. Later, hundreds of them paraded through Carlstadt and East Rutherford to protest the Democratic presidential nomination of Al Smith, Catholic governor of New York.

A Franciscan priest stood defiantly in his robes on the steps of St. Joseph's Church in East Rutherford as they passed by.

During this period the county's industrial complex grew and diversified still further. The stock market crash and resulting depression brought a sharp business decline, but by 1935 industrial employment and production statistics had both risen above their 1929 levels. Centers for textiles were in Garfield, Lodi and East Paterson where mills and bleaching and dyeing establishments spilled over from Paterson and Passaic. In Edgewater, among others, there were Alcoa aluminum, National Sugar Refining and a huge Ford assembly plant. Many communities had some industry. In Bogogta there were three large paper mills. In East Rutherford was Becton Dickinson and Company, manufacturers of surgical instruments, and in Mahwah, the American Brake Shoe and Foundry Company.

The county's labor history was marked by a number of strikes which attracted attention nationwide. In 1926 Bergen textile mills were closed for months by a strike started in Passaic. The owners and managers argued that the participation of radicals and communists in support of the strike represented an open threat to the political and economic system. The strike leaders charged police brutality. The textile industry was shaken by a strike again in 1933, but in some ways the most significant labor disturbances of the period came at the Air Associates plant in Teterboro where in 1941, after drawn out confrontation between the CIO organizers and an intransigent

management, President Roosevelt decided to use his legal authorization to seize the plant in the interests of national defense and to operate it under the supervision of military personnel. The incident threatened labor peace up and down the East Coast.

In the broad sweep of American political history perhaps the key development of the twentieth century has been the broadening of the role of the government to include social and economic planning and the delivery of all sorts of social services. Historian John Cunningham notes that in November 1930, as the depression deepened in New Jersey, Bergen County was the first in the state to take action by offering road work to the unemployed. One thousand men were happy to put in seven hard hours and take home three dollars to their families. In 1934 there were sixty-six hundred families on Bergen's relief rolls, a situation which would remain serious throughout the decade. Bergen played host to two CCC (Civil Conservation Corps) camps and benefited from a generous series of PWA (Public Works Administration) and WPA (Works Progress Administration) federal projects. In 1940 the *Bergen Record* summed up some of them: 275 miles of roadway, thirty-eight miles of storm and sanitary sewers, sixteen new buildings including a new bus terminal in Hackensack (since demolished) and Borough Hall in Closter, and the expansion or renovation of seventy-one school buildings. In addition there were efforts at mosquito control, sewing room programs to make clothes for the needy, shade tree planting, mural painting in public

buildings, and the writing of municipal histories.

Bergen's traditional Republican majorities assured that the New Deal would have its political critics, but a few went beyond lawful opposition. The KKK was still active, especially when the CCC brought in groups of blacks to work on projects. In January of 1934 secret meetings of fascist sympathizers in Garfield, Lodi, Ridgefield Park and Hackensack cheered Arthur J. Smith, the man who, according to the *Bergen Record*, they wanted "to make dictator of America." The *Record* reported that many of the names associated with the Hackensack meeting were Italian, and that Smith apologized for addressing them in English. Although German-Americans were forced to restrict the activities of their social and political organizations during World War I, the Bund left its mark on the 1930s, in favor of Hitler's Germany and opposed to American social policy.

In 1939 a committee of the American Legion in Haworth was appointed to examine the local schoolbooks for "socialist dogma." Such campaigns against the free exchange of ideas were not uncommon at the time. A local history published twenty years later referred to the incident as "an historic intellectual struggle." Surely North Jersey's best known congressman of the period would have agreed. J. Parnell Thomas, elected to Congress from the Seventh District (Bergen County) in 1937, made a national reputation for himself on the House Committee on UnAmerican Activities. He resigned from office in 1950 after his conviction for payroll padding.

In large measure, calmer and wiser heads prevailed. The 1930s in Bergen County saw a gradual awakening to the need for careful planning of future development. Local zoning ordinances were discussed in many communities and passed in a few, as ways to set up guidelines for controlling the development boom which people regarded as inevitable once the depression was over. Teaneck was one community which led the way in local administrative reform. In 1930 they were the first to change from a township committee to a city manager form of government, and their first administrator Paul A. Voelker set the tone for fiscal responsibility and thoughtful community planning that professional municipal administrators everywhere would seek to follow in the decade ahead.

As the county marshalled its efforts to assist in the Second World War, it was evident that significant changes had taken place in Bergen since the last great struggle. Again, Bergen made its contribution to the home front, selling bonds, collecting scrap materials, living with the rationing of food supplies and gasoline; and again they sent their sons to war by the thousands. Mrs. Leo Martin, long time teacher and principal at the junior high school in New Milford, had a special feeling for many of them. Throughout the war she maintained a faithful correspondence with the alumni of her school who were serving in the armed forces—some 375 of them.

The original design of the George Washington Bridge drawn by famed architect Cass Gilbert called for the towers to be faced in stone. This concept was abandoned, however, when the beauty and drama of the steel structure work became apparent upon its completion. Le Corbusier, celebrated French architect, declared it to be the most beautiful bridge in the world. This view is from the New Jersey side, looking east over a hazy Hudson River. Courtesy Newark Public Library

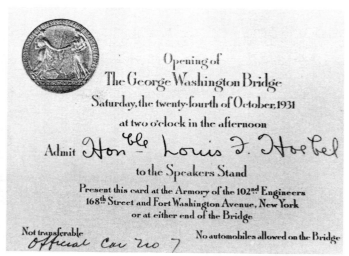

The Honorable Louis F. Hoebel was one of the
dignitaries admitted to the speakers' stand at
the dedication of the bridge, October 24,
1931. Courtesy Fort Lee Public Library

Gilbert's original design was reproduced for
the Architectural Exhibition held at Newark
under the auspices of the New Jersey Chapter
of the American Institute of Architects and the
New Jersey Society of Architects. From The
American Architect, February 5, 1927

New York's governor Franklin Delano
Roosevelt spoke from the gaily decorated
grandstand erected in the center of the George
Washington Bridge for the dedication
ceremonies. In the foreground is the white silk

ribbon which he and New Jersey's governor
Morgan Larson cut while airplanes flew in
formation overhead; river boats tooted below;
and the band played the "Star-Spangled
Banner." A project of the New York Port

Authority, the bridge supplied a necessary
automotive link between the New England
states and the rest of the United States.
Courtesy Newark Public Library

Military men marching over bridges traditionally break step to avoid the stress that a measured cadence may impose upon the structure of the span. In a gesture of confidence in the strength of the George Washington Bridge, participants in the military parade which accompanied the dedication ceremonies abandoned the standard procedure, and remained in perfect step along the length of the bridge. *Courtesy Newark Public Library*

Anticipating the expected real estate boom in the wake of the George Washington Bridge, an ambitious young developer, Charles Reis, turned one hundred acres of farmland in Wood-Ridge into "Sunshine City," an early adventure in mass-produced housing. In this aerial view of 1928, rows of single family homes line the new streets of Wood-Ridge, stretching westward from Hackensack Street in the middle foreground. The open land beyond the tract would later house Curtiss Wright's aircraft engine plant, built in 1942. *Courtesy History of Wood-Ridge Committee*

So-called colonial homes under construction in Sunshine City circa 1928. *Courtesy Newark Public Library*

The apartment house, bastion of urbanization, appeared with increasing frequency in the more densely settled areas of the county. Corporate ownership was sometimes based in New York City, as in the case of the Englewood Garden Apartments pictured above. Courtesy Teaneck Public Library

The real estate firm promoting West Englewood Manor dramatically highlighted the extensive tract's alleged direct connection with the proposed new bridge. The small enclosed captions refer to convenient train, bus and trolley routes, including the "new vehicular tunnel" at upper right. West Englewood is a section of Teaneck lying north of Route 4. "The prize property of Bergen County" was developed by a firm from New York. Courtesy Teaneck Public Library

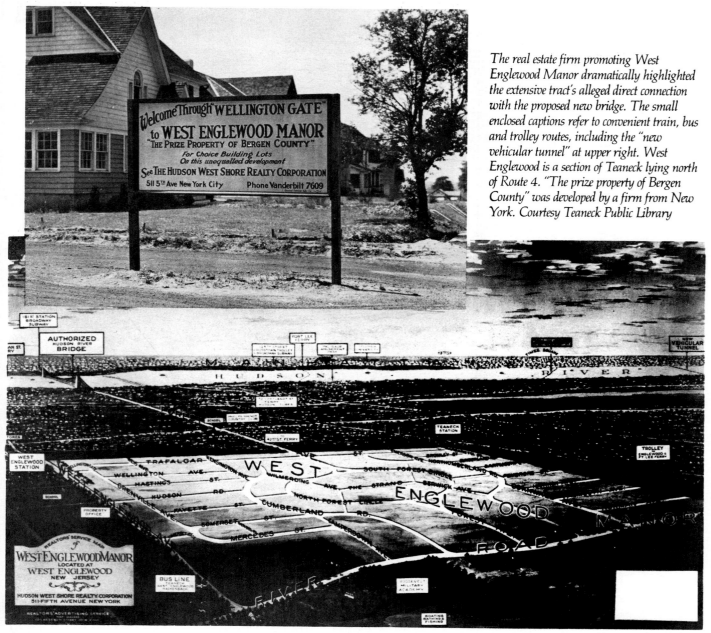

Interior of house at West Englewood Manor incorporates details of design popular in the 1920s, particularly the center chandelier and the ubiquitous wall sconce. "Model homes" were often opened for display and provided popular outings for many a Bergen County housewife interested in the latest developments in kitchen furnishings or the newest colors in bathroom tile. Courtesy Teaneck Public Library

Although so-called colonial designs (a broad realty term for almost any two-story house) dominated at West Englewood Manor, at least one model reflected the Spanish colonial revival current in California and Florida during this period. Courtesy Teaneck Public Library

Real estate developers offered a variety of styles to tempt New Yorkers to relocate on the other side of the George Washington Bridge. The page pictured is from a Fort Lee brochure which advertised, "Only twenty minutes from Times Square." Courtesy Fort Lee Public Library

RADBURN

Radburn, one of the first planned communities in the United States, anticipated the average American's dependence upon the automobile. In 1929 architects and planners of the City Housing Corporation deliberately set out to create an environment which would minimize the impact of wheeled vehicles in a community designed to provide housing, open space, and opportunities for recreation and cultural growth. Now over fifty years old, Radburn is still a self-contained community whose residents generally agree that the plan still works. Courtesy of New Jersey Bell

Architect's sketch of the Radburn master plan illustrates the "super-blocks" of clustered housing which limited access to automobiles while providing open space and walkways for recreation and communication. Only two super-blocks had actually been constructed when the Depression stifled home buying and put an end to further development. Courtesy Paterson Museum

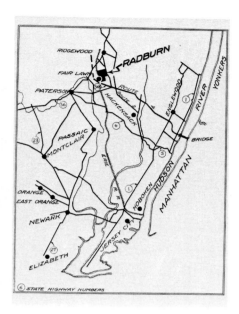

Located in Fair Lawn "ten miles from Manhattan as the crow flies" eleven miles from the George Washington Bridge, and twenty-five minutes by train from Jersey City, Radburn's promotion was also tailored to commuter concerns. The highway on the map marked "Route 2," is the forerunner of Route 17. Courtesy Paterson Museum

An evidently unplanned path leads to Radburn's Plaza Building on the corner of Fair Lawn Avenue and Plaza Road. In addition to its role as a commercial center, the Plaza Building was also the focus of cultural and social activities, accommodating conferences, meetings, dances, musical and dramatic presentations, and courses in adult education. Among its other uses, the tower clock was relied upon in alloting reservations on the tennis court two blocks away. Courtesy Paterson Museum

Radburn's homes face the communal walkway and the front lawns of opposite neighbors. A typical homeowner would have been a thirty-five year old college graduate employed in business or a profession, earning between $3,000 and $5,000 per year. Three times out of four his wife would have been a college graduate also, and a homemaker. Courtesy Paterson Museum

In Radburn's model home, the latest model cabinets, sink and appliances awaited the 1932 housewife. Upstairs, spindles and ruffles decorated a feminine bedroom. Courtesy Paterson Museum

Radburn's housing mix included apartment houses framed here by a connecting archway similar to the one in the rear and at the right. The striped awnings provided relief from the summer sun before the advent of air conditioning. Courtesy Paterson Museum

Except for the cul-de-sacs behind the houses, automobiles were restricted to highways surrounding "the super-blocks," and carried over the walkways by arches of concrete and stone. A child could walk to school from any home in Radburn without crossing a road. In the early thirties approximately one-quarter of Radburn's population was juvenile, and half of these were pre-school. Courtesy Paterson Museum

In the 1920s, trains and trolleys were still a favored means of transportation. Here a crowd of travelers awaits to board a train at the Ridgewood Station. Courtesy The Ridgewood NEWSpapers

The crossing gates are closed as an Erie passenger train pulls into Rutherford's Station Square in the early 1930s. The small white tower at center would have housed a patrolman directing traffic. The engine is blocking a view of Park Avenue in East Rutherford, and at right center, that borough's venerable Erie Hotel, lately destroyed by fire. Courtesy Newark Public Library

By 1921, the New Jersey and New York Railroad was part of the Erie system. According to the fare schedule reproduced here, Bergen County commuters paid between $7.26 and $11.03 for a monthly ticket. Nineteen trains daily ran in each direction between New York City and towns in the Pascack Valley. Notice the war revenue tax still in force three years after the cessation of hostilities. Courtesy New Jersey Room, Fairleigh Dickinson University, Rutherford

Trolleys of the Hudson River Line wait in the Public Service Yard at Edgewater Ferry in 1937 overlooked by one of Bergen County's prime trolley destinations, Palisades Amusement Park on the cliffs above. New Yorkers would pack the park on summer evenings and weekends. The ferry ride and trolley trip up the Palisades were all part of the fun. Courtesy North Jersey Chapter, National Railway Historical Society

Tenafly railroad station was the last stop for trolleys of the Englewood Line. The return trip carried passengers to the 125th Street ferry. Attributed to architect J. Cleveland Cady, the station now appears on the National List of Historic Places. William R. Agnew photo, courtesy Virginia Mosley, Tenafly Borough Historian

Hudson River trolley photographed in 1933 at First Street and Central Avenue, Hackensack, carries the blue eagle of the NRA, Franklin D. Roosevelt's effort to stimulate a lagging economy. Courtesy North Jersey Chapter, National Railway Historical Society

At the Newark terminal circa 1930, suburban passengers wait for Public Service buses. The truck-like vehicles could accommodate thirty people on their rattan seats. Increasing public acceptance of the bus led to a gradual phasing-out of trolley lines. The turning point came in 1929 when, for the first time, buses carried more passengers than did the trolley lines. Bus No. 102, recently renumbered No. 76, still carries passengers from Newark to Hackensack as listed on the third panel to the right above. Courtesy Public Service Electric and Gas Co.

Public Service bus driver accepts his bonus for accident-free bus operation during 1929. Center wall panel lists drivers for the company's Bergen County routes. Courtesy Public Service Electric and Gas Co.

Many communities supported active retailing areas. Hackensack's Main Street was the natural focus for South Bergen shoppers, accessible by trolley, bus and automobile, and circa 1925, from this postcard view, parking was evidently not a problem. Notice the trolley tracks bisecting Main Street. Postcard courtesy Johnson Free Public Library

Before the advent of the electric refrigerator, the ice man was a familiar figure at many a Bergen County home, balancing a large cake of ice on his leather clad shoulder. To supply the wooden ice-boxes often located on a drafty back porch, the ice was harvested from local ponds in wintertime and stored in ice houses kept cold by their contents through the following summer. The photograph depicts relatively sophisticated motorized ice-cutting equipment operated at Garrison's Pond in Ramsey circa 1923, with the Garrison Ice House in the background. Courtesy Home and School News

The winter's fuel supply was delivered down a chute inserted through a basement window, and entered the waiting coal bin with a satisfying swish and rumble which never failed to fascinate the youngest members of the family watching from the nearest window. The dump truck pictured here modernized the former procedure in which the coal arrived on a flatbed truck loaded with double-handled canvas bags. Courtesy Paterson Museum

OBEL'S MARKET
295 SEMEL AVE.
GARFIELD, N.J.

The local market supplied basic foods, personal service, and often home delivery for telephoned orders. In the lower view of Obel's market in Garfield photographed in 1937, two butchers wait to cut meat to order with deft strokes of sharp knives. The sawdust on the floor would be renewed each day as a sanitary measure. The photographs were taken by the Service Butcher Fixture and Supply Company of Paterson which had just installed the new equipment. Courtesy Paterson Museum

This Hackensack resident uses Timken *oil heating in another house, too*

Mr. Bogert's satisfaction with Timken oil heating is such that he has installed it in *two* houses—the one pictured above, and another one equally attractive, located near by.

In his own words, ".... Since installation, everything has worked to our perfect satisfaction, each burner starting promptly from the thermostat at required temperature and shutting off when the required heat is attained ..... There is scarcely any noise ..... no odor, dust or soot in the cellar or elsewhere in either house.''

Why not put the responsibility of the Timken-Detroit Company, builders of axles for the finest automobiles, behind your proposed oil burner purchase? Why not obtain the benefits of reliable, permanent factory branch service such as you get when you invest in a Timken Oil Burner?

Come and see the Timken in operation. Even at this time of year, we can install one in your present hot air furnace or steam or hot water plant with such rapidity that you will experience no discomfort before the burner is in and working. Write or telephone for our most interesting free oil burner book.

THE TIMKEN-DETROIT COMPANY, DETROIT, MICHIGAN
(Subsidiary of The Timken-Detroit Axle Co.)

Factory Branch and Showroom: 354 Main Street, East Orange, N. J.
(Opposite D. L. & W. Station) Telephone Orange 700—Open evenings until 9 o'clock

— SALES OFFICES —

217 East Front St., Plainfield, N. J.
 Telephone 6432

327 Main St., Hackensack, N. J.
 Telephone 5672

445 Parkway Ave., Trenton, N. J.
 Telephone 7-5735

The Timken Oil Burner may be seen at the New York showrooms of Socony Burner Corporation, 9 East 40th Street and 24 Broadway

54 South St., Morristown, N. J.
 Telephone 2717-W

5 Colt St., Room 504, Paterson, N. J.
 Telephone Sherwood 8610

D. L. Byrd., Red Bank, N. J.
 Conover Lane, Telephone 821-J

TIMKEN
OIL BURNER
"WHO MAKES IT MAKES A DIFFERENCE"
Listed as Standard by the Underwriters' Laboratories

The owner of this Hackensack home profiled by the Timken oil burner company in a 1926 issue of Charm *magazine, praised the new unit for its convenience and cleanliness. From* Charm, *November 1926*

The Mascari Brothers truck was a familiar sight on the streets of Ridgewood. The Paterson firm had been selling fresh fruit and vegetables door-to-door since the early 1900s. Courtesy The Ridgewood NEWSpapers

Fred Lang's new delivery truck, photographed in 1923, advertised telephone connections but did not provide a telephone number. Presumably "Central" knew how to ring him. Courtesy Fred W. Quantmeyer, Sr., Harrington Park Borough Historian

Home deliveries decreased as the corner grocery store faced increasing competition from a new concept of merchandising which emphasized self-service, speed, and economy; anticipating the modern supermarket. Prices posted in this Ridgewood A&P in September 1941 increased sharply during the next four years in spite of the efforts of the U.S. Office of Price Administration to curb inflation. Courtesy Paterson Museum

Wing walkers from Gates Flying Circus wave from their wooden biplane moored in Teterboro's marshy acres. Springtime flooding at the airport was common until the installation of sewer water pumps in 1946. The hanger at the left of the picture was owned by Wright Aeronautical Corporation which tested and installed Wright Whirlwind engines at Teterboro. Courtesy The Ridgewood NEWSpapers

Aviation buffs assembled at Teterboro Airport in 1927, to watch a performance of Gates Flying Circus, based at Teterboro from 1926 to 1929. Dressed in riding breeches and boots, flying helmets and long white scarves, the stunt pilots and aerial acrobats of the Flying Circus barnstormed all over the United States until new federal safety regulations in 1929 put an end to their daredevil exploits. Their shows at Teterboro slowed traffic for miles north and south on Route 2 (now Route 17). Courtesy Newark Public Library

Bergen County's flying police chief, Peter J. Siccardi, stands at center as the county's aerial police made their debut on May 22, 1929 at Teterboro Airport. First of its kind in the United States, the squad was organized by Siccardi, an aviation enthusiast who allegedly took to the air in 1927 to direct 200 traffic policemen by semaphore when crowds converged on Teterboro Airport during the First National Air Show. Only two of the pilots were actually on the rolls of the county police. The rest, who served without pay, included famous flyers Bernt Balchen and Clyde Pangborn. Wright test pilot Leo Allen was also a member of the squad. Courtesy Newark Public Library

Rutherford Yacht Club's first motorboat regatta on the Passaic River attracted this holiday crowd on July 4, 1928. Organized the previous March to encourage boating and other water sports, the club's headquarters, pictured here, was constructed on River Road in Rutherford at the foot of West Newell Avenue in the spring of the same year. After an apparent bankruptcy in 1936, the building was converted to commercial use and is currently a candidate for consideration as a national historic site. Courtesy Newark Public Library

The formal opening of Rutherford's Rivoli Theater on April 22, 1922 was attended by 2,000 people who admired the melodious pipe organ and the sparkling crystal chandelier which was so large that some apprehensive Rutherfordians avoided sitting directly underneath. The opening bill presented Constance Tallmadge in Polly of the Follies and Buster Keaton in Playhouse. The manager pledged that the theater would present "only clean wholesome pictures of the highest order." The theater has been lately renovated to emerge as the William Carlos Williams Center for the Performing Arts. Courtesy Meadowlands Museum

WOHELO; WOrk, HEalth, LOve, was the motto of these Ramsey Camp Fire Girls, members of a national organization introduced circa 1912. Camp Fire Girls learned Indian lore and customs, adopting Indian-style garments and beaded headbands which they made for ceremonial meetings around a campfire. The young lady second from right is wearing knickers, a sportswear fashion popular during the 1920s. Courtesy Home and Store News

The Rotary Club of Midland Park held its inaugural luncheon at the Pomander Inn in Ridgewood, January 3, 1927. As part of Rotary International, a service organization instituted in Chicago in 1905, Rotarians have traditionally been active in civic and community pursuits, particularly those which encourage good citizenship among young people. The members pictured here would have been drawn from the business and professional men of Midland Park. Courtesy Midland Park Historical Society

During the presidential election campaign of 1924, Ramsey Republicans unfurled yet another imposing banner on West Main Street. Walter Edge, formerly governor of New Jersey, was running for his second term as United States senator. The brooms decorating the support poles indicate Republican confidence in a "clean sweep." Courtesy Home and Store News

The Republican Club of Hasbrouck Heights operated from a storefront on the Boulevard during the presidential campaign of 1932. Although Franklin D. Roosevelt was the first Democratic presidential candidate to carry Bergen County since Wilson's second term, Hasbrouck Heights voters continued to support the Republican ticket all the way. Courtesy Hasbrouck Heights Public Library

The Kohbertz mansion in Wood-Ridge served for a short time in the 1920s as a headquarters for the Ku Klux Klan. Designed in the Second Empire style, the twenty-room mansion featured a fifteen-foot hallway of black marble. Built in the 1870s by Frederick Kohbertz, a local land developer, the estate occupied three acres on the highest point of Wood-Ridge, overlooking both the Hackensack and the Passaic Valleys. After functioning as a restaurant, and perhaps a speakeasy, the mansion was razed by the borough in 1940 following a disastrous fire. Courtesy History of Wood-Ridge Committee

Teterboro Airport played an important role in the development of America's fledging aircraft industry. Sparked by the inventive genius of Anthony Fokker, Dutch aircraft designer and manufacturer, Fokker tri-motors with Wright aircraft engines installed at Teterboro, gained fame in the historic long-distance flights of the late twenties and early thirties, paving the way for commercial aviation in the United States. In this early photograph, Fokker sits at the wheel of one of his experimental aircraft, circa 1911. When he began operations in Teterboro, Fokker was already known as the designer of the triplane made famous during World War I by Manfred von Richtofen, the celebrated "Red Baron" of the German air force. Courtesy Hasbrouck Heights Public Library

Fokker's unique steel-tubed fuselages are in evidence in this view of planes in production at his Teterboro plant. The Dutch manufacturer acquired the vacant hangars of the Whitteman-Lewis Aircraft Company, established in 1918 by a family of aviation pioneers who went bankrupt building the "biggest bombing ship in the world" for the U.S. Army. By 1929 Fokker's factory at Teterboro and its subsidiary near Passaic were producing an airplane every week. Courtesy Hasbrouck Heights Public Library

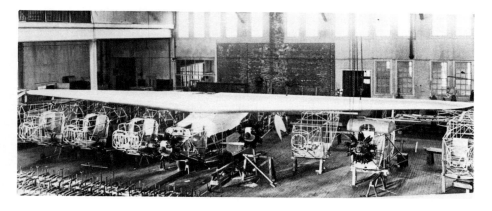

A Fokker floatplane carried Amelia Earhart on her historic flight across the Atlantic in 1928. She is shown here at Teterboro Airport with her mechanic, Ed Gorski, and advisor Bernt Balchen. A co-pilot and mechanic on the Fokker 32, an early commercial airliner, Gorski operated Teterboro Airport during the Depression years of the 1930s. Balchen, Richard Byrd's chief pilot on his expedition to Antartica, became the first man to fly over the South Pole. A lieutenant in the Norwegian Naval Air Force and some-time resident of Hasbrouck Heights, Bernt Balchen was an honorary member of the Bergen County Chamber of Commerce. Courtesy Hasbrouck Heights Public Library

Bernt Balchen was also the pilot on Commander Richard Byrd's Fokker tri-motor America, the third aircraft to cross the Atlantic after Lindberg's historic flight. Heavy fog over the airport aborted their landing at Le Bourget Airport near Paris. Instead, they were forced into the ocean near Ver-sur-Mer, well known to the next generation of Americans as Omaha Beach. Courtesy Hasbrouck Heights Public Library

One-half of the population of Teterboro threw up their hats to cheer the flag-raising at their municipal building which also served as Clarence Chamberlain's modest home. Teterboro residents were celebrating their native son's non-stop flight to Germany in 1927, two weeks after Lindberg's solo flight to Paris. More than any other famous aviator associated with Teterboro Airport, Chamberlain was one of Bergen County's true aviation pioneers. He lived and worked at Teterboro over two decades, at one point serving as mayor of the miniscule community. Courtesy Newark Public Library

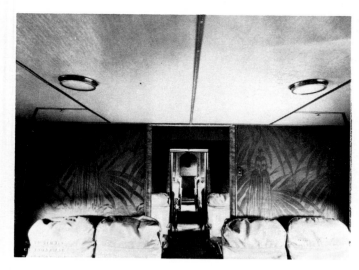

Interior and exterior views of the F. 32, an early commercial airliner built at Teterboro, New Jersey. The last Fokker of commercial design built in the United States, the plane had thirty-two seats in four compartments, and could serve as a sixteen-berth sleeper at night. Pan-American Airlines used the F. 32 on its first passenger flight from Key West to Havana, Cuba. Courtesy Hasbrouck Heights Public Library

Sketches of the proposed George Washington Bridge highlight a promotional brochure for Bergen County's first Industrial Exposition. Approximately 2,000 persons attended opening exercises during which they were addressed by Mayor Vanderwart and entertained by the Bergen County American Legion Band. Exhibitors shared tents on a lot at Moore Street and Demarest Place. Two tents were dedicated to the latest model automobiles. The main tent accommodated eighty booths, "displaying exhibits of numerous local and national advertisers," including the Johnson Free Public Library. The Bergen Evening Record reported that "in keeping with the respectability of the firms exhibiting," no gambling wheels or games of chance would be allowed. Courtesy Bergen County Historical Society

The Ford Motor Company's assembly plant at Edgewater began operations in 1935. This photograph dramatically illustrates the concentration of transportation facilities which made Edgewater a prime industrial location in the first half of the twentieth century. Materials and products were easily shipped by rail and by water. Ferries and trolleys provided easy egress for those workers who did not commute by automobile from the surrounding urban areas. With the post-war construction of express highways and the resulting increase in truck transportation, Edgewater's industries declined. Ford moved assembly operations to Mahwah in 1955. Courtesy New Jersey Historical Society

Shad fishermen are mending nets along the
Hudson River in the spring of 1940.
Generations of fishermen from the small
settlements along the Palisades have harvested
boat loads of silvery shad as the saltwater fish
made their springtime journey up the river to
their spawning grounds farther north.
Although the season was short, a shad
fisherman could realize a tidy sum during the
six weeks when the fish were running well. In
the second photograph, later Edgewater
fishermen admire a prize specimen, handsome
enough to have graced one of Mayor Henry
Wissel's annual dinners for Republican
mayors and invited guests. The industry has
now declined, suffering from increased river
pollution and considerable attrition of the shad
roe in their spawning grounds. Courtesy
Newark Public Library and Edgewater
Public Library

Before the merger which created the United Piece Dye Works in Lodi in 1903, Mill B had been the former Boettger Piece Dye Works, built in 1896 in part upon the site occupied for years by Robert Rennie, Lodi's most famous entrepreneur. In 1875 Rennie closed the calico print works he had established fifty years before, to engage in the manufacture of chemicals and dye stuffs, setting the stage for Lodi's burgeoning new industry. In the photograph above a workman feeds cloth into the huge dyeing vat of the United Piece Dye Works...Courtesy Paterson Museum

...and it comes out here. Courtesy Paterson Museum

TEXTILE STRIKERS STRUGGLE ON

The Sheriff of Bergen County has read the riot ac
　　But this will never break the strike!

Halls have been closed against the strikers!
　　But this will never break the strike!

The police have clubbed men, women and childre
on the picket lines.
　　But this will never break our strike!

Organizer Weisbord is in jail! They want $30,000 ba
They want to arrest him again the minute he leav
jail. But this will not break the strike!

NOTHING WILL BREAK THIS STRIKE. All THREE SHIFTS have STRUCK to BT
OUT OF THE MILLS, and that settles it. We, the strikers, will stay out of the mills unti
bosses get some sense! If the bosses think they are going to bluff us, they are mistaken. I
think they are going to scare us with their guns and clubs and riot acts, they are mistaken.
And the police will never make us do unlawful things. The police, the bosses, all
bosses' friends have been aching to have a striker do an act of violence.

THE BOSSES HAVE A MONOPOLY ON VIOLENCE: It is the bosses who
se workers, and by violence deny free speech and free assemblage.

IT IS THE BOSSES WHO USE VIOLENCE and they use it BECAUSE TH
RE WEAKENING! They know that up to now the workers have played a better hand
hey have. The strikers have gotten the best of them. And so now the mill bosses think
ey can club the workers back into the mills.

NEVER!! Let the bosses play all their tricks. WE WILL NEVER GO BACK
THE MILLS UNTIL THE BOSSES TREAT US LIKE HUMAN BEINGS and talk with our
anization about our grievances. We have always stood ready to talk with the bosses about our
ands. The bosses have never been ready.

THE BOSSES WILL HAVE TO TALK TO US! They w
ave to do this or the textile mills will not run a minute. W
ARE GOING TO WIN! We shall win no matter what t
osses do or say.

Strikers! Stand by the Union! Stand by Weisbor
Stand by all our Brothers in Jail! Stand by o
Principles! Stand United for Victory!

United Front Committee of Textile Workers

The violence which marked the 1926 strike of the Passaic woolen industry spilled over into Bergen County as this broadside illustrates. United Piece Dye workers in Lodi, along with weavers from Dundee Worsted in what is now Elmwood Park, walked the picket lines during a strike called by the United Front Committee Textile Workers, an organization led by communist activist Alfred Weisbord.

Strike demands centered upon wages and hours and union recognition. After eight months of confrontation, the strike was settled through the mediation of local residents and clergy. Workers at Lodi were the last to return to work, formally ending the strike February 28, 1927. Courtesy Special Collections, Alexander Library, Rutgers University

Under the aegis of the American Federation of Labor, textile workers walked out again in a six week strike in 1933 protesting low wages and illegal working conditions, and demanding once more, union recognition. Men shown in the photograph are picketing the United Piece Dye Works in Lodi. Over 14,000 dyers in the Paterson area were on strike, idling Bergen County dye plants in Lodi, Fair Lawn and what is now East Paterson. The final settlement included a minimum wage of twenty-three dollars for a forty-hour week, and the right to collective bargaining. Courtesy Newark Public Library

An attractive picket in a borrowed raincoat encouraged the union flag-bearer engaged in the lengthy and bitter struggle between the United Auto Workers and Air Associates in the fall of 1941. The Teterboro firm had received more than five million dollars in defense contracts to produce retractable landing gear for British and American war planes. Courtesy Newark Public Library

Soldiers challenge a car at the entrance to Air Associates in Teterboro after the Army assumed operation of the plant following Franklin D. Roosevelt's order of October 30, 1941. Courtesy Newark Public Library

CWA workers dig out a Hackensack street following a thirty-six hour snowfall in February 1934. The Civil Works Administration was a federal program which provided jobs for the unemployed and for the able-bodied on relief. Workers were placed on the federal payroll and paid the minimum wage. The program was originally conceived to help an increasingly desperate section of the nation's unemployed through the Depression winter of 1933-34, which proved to be unusually severe. The February blizzard described above was accompanied by forty-five mile winds, and was Bergen County's third serious storm of the winter. Courtesy The Record

The Civilian Conservation Corps was another New Deal program which employed men between seventeen and twenty-eight years old to conserve and develop the nation's natural resources. Two camps in Bergen County enrolled more than 300 men, largely from Bergen and Hudson counties. This early view shows the CCC encampment at Teterboro before the men were housed in barracks. Budget restrictions forced the closing of the camp in 1938. Courtesy Hasbrouck Heights Public Library

Alarmed by the cost of CWA, the Roosevelt administration abandoned the program in the spring of 1934 and substituted relief measures such as the Emergency Relief Administration (ERA) and the better-known Works Progress Administration (WPA) funded also by state and local governments. The workmen shown above maintaining roads in Tenafly circa 1934-35 were undoubtedly working under one of these programs. Photo by William R. Agnew, courtesy of Virginia Mosley, Tenafly Borough Historian

The CCC camp at Teterboro was sponsored by the Bergen County Mosquito Extermination Commission. Consequently, the men employed there spent long hours digging drainage ditches or building flood dykes and gates for mosquito control. They operated in the Hackensack Meadows, Secaucus, and Overpeck Creek. The photograph above graphically illustrates the nature of their work. Black companies were the first and the last units to occupy the camp at Teterboro. Courtesy The Record

The intersection of Route 2 (now Route 17) and Paterson Plank Road in Carlstadt illustrates the local traffic which motorists encountered on the early north-south artery before construction in the early 1930s introduced limited access to some sections of the highway. To facilitate interstate travel, particularly that of military vehicles, Route 2's numbering was changed in 1942 to correspond with New York State's Route 17 with which it connects. This 1940 view looks eastward along Paterson Plank Road into the Hackensack Meadows. The bus at left has just passed the Carlstadt railroad station and is bound for Paterson along the earlier trolley route. Courtesy Paterson Museum

The Teaneck section of Route 4, the final link in that highway through Bergen County, was opened July 29, 1932. Since the route ran through a residential area of Teaneck, the township successfully discouraged commercial development along the strip by buying land on either side. Route 4 was the first of a number of highways planned to cope with the increase in traffic generated by the George Washington Bridge. Courtesy Teaneck Public Library

South Bergen motorists will recognize this dramatic aerial view of the intersection of Routes 46 and 17 at the northern edge of Hasbrouck Heights. Considered an early marvel of traffic engineering, a photograph of the intersection appeared on the map issued by the New Jersey Highway Department in 1941. Opened in 1934 as Route 6, the new highway was also designed to funnel traffic from the George Washington Bridge to the Delaware River, and was completed through Bergen County by 1937. The route designation was changed in 1953 during a general renumbering of all New Jersey highways. Courtesy Hasbrouck Heights Public Library

Pleasure Land on Doty Road bordering Route 202 in Oakland was one of a number of popular beaches along the Ramapo River. Swimmers now have a choice of two swimming pools located across the road from the old swimming hole. Courtesy Oakland Historical Society

SWIM & PICNIC
at
Springrove Beach

Midland Park, N. J.

Social activities tended toward the convivial and, at least during the Depression, the inexpensive. Before the proliferation of back-yard swimming pools, family picnics would include a swim at local watering places such as Springrove Beach, located at Paterson and Cross Avenues in Midland Park. Initially known as Morrow Park, the swimming facility was created by damming Wagaraw Brook. Adult admission was fifteen cents. Courtesy Special Collections, Alexander Library, Rutgers University

Anona Lake in Upper Saddle River was formed by damming the west branch of the Saddle River. Regular visitors who returned each time to the same picnic area, embellished their tables for comfort and convenience. Note the canopy and icebox at the table in the foreground. Courtesy William Yeomans, Upper Saddle River

169

All seats were reserved for the grand opening
of the Warner Theatre in Ridgewood in
1932. The movie, which featured Warren
Williams in The Dark House, was
followed by personal appearances of show
business luminaries, including child star
Mitzi Green who did an imitation of George
Arliss. Master of Ceremonies Jack Haley
read a congratulatory "telegraph" from
Hollywood from the three Warner brothers,
whose portraits grace the ticket shown above.
Courtesy The Ridgewood NEWSpapers

After the movies one might stop at the local
soda fountain for ice cream or coke.
Gurewitz's candy store in Hackensack had
room for four customers at its counter in
1935. Courtesy Paterson Museum

Small boys continued to provide for their own
entertainment. The photograph shows a
sandlot baseball team in Wood-Ridge circa
1930, before the advent of the Little League.
Courtesy History of Wood-Ridge Committee

In 1932, Harrington Park boys in knee pants celebrated the end of Prohibition in Bergen County with a spontaneous parade. Courtesy Fred W. Quantmeyer, Sr., Harrington Park Borough Historian

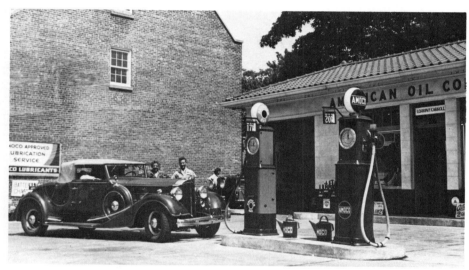

For young men, ownership of an automobile was traditionally one of the rites of passage as well as virtual guarantee of popularity with the opposite sex. This photograph of a 1934 Packard convertible taken at the Amoco Gas Station in Tenafly is from the collection of William R. Agnew, the car's owner, who is barely visible in the interior. Courtesy Virginia Mosley, Tenafly Borough Historian

Public Service sponsored the float pictured above in the parade celebrating Englewood's thirty-fifth anniversary in 1934. The Victorian housewife stands between her antiquated gas range and icebox, while her liberated counterpart relaxes with a magazine next to an electric refrigerator. The wringer washing machine exhibited in the store window retailed for $79. Courtesy Public Service Gas and Electric Co.

Many communities in Bergen County were within a short ferry ride to New York City with its multiple cultural activities which provided entertainment and education for young and old. From the formality of their dress, one might conjecture that the boys in this photograph may have been returning from a family outing in Manhattan. Perhaps their mother served as photographer as they climbed Route 5 in Edgewater, their backs turned to the panoramic view of the New York skyline, dominated by Riverside Memorial Church. Courtesy Edgewater Public Library

A precursor of the family room, the recreation area in this Palisades Park cellar shared space with the home's heating system in 1938. Courtesy Paterson Museum

Other families found imaginative uses for a limited backyard. This patio area for summer entertaining was created in Cliffside Park circa 1940. Richard Averill Smith photograph courtesy New Jersey Historical Society

Bergen County's middle class often chose attractive custom-built homes such as the Hackensack residence shown here, designed by architect Wesley Bessell circa 1935. The patterned carpet in the living room draws together a diversity of styles which reflect the owners' eclectic taste in furniture and creates an atmosphere of hominess and comfort. The screened porch would provide a welcome retreat on summer afternoons and evenings. Architectural plans provided for only one bathroom. Notice the convenient walk-through pantry which connects kitchen and dining room, and the ample provision of closet space, especially on the second floor. All photographs by Richard Averill Smith. Courtesy New Jersey Historical Society

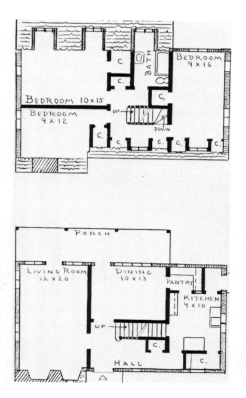

Early in the twentieth century, Englewood became the suburb of choice for such prominent members of New York City's financial community as Thomas Lamont and Dwight W. Morrow, both associated with the firm of J. P. Morgan. Morrow was United States ambassador to Mexico in 1927 and also served with distinction in state and local civic affairs. The Morrow estate pictured here became the center of national interest at the time of daughter Anne Morrow's marriage to the popular hero Charles A. Lindberg. Reporters again beseiged the gates after the couple's first child was kidnapped from their south Jersey home in 1932. *Courtesy Newark Public Library*

Seward Prosser, a vice-president of the Astor Trust, was raised in Englewood, attended Smith's private school for boys and played first base for the Englewood Field Club. This Prosser house interior photographed in 1929 shows the drawing room attractively furnished in a mixture of French and English furniture in the eighteenth century style. *Mattie Edwards Hewitt photograph courtesy New Jersey Historical Society*

Drawing room of the Darlington Mansion in Mahwah as it appeared before the auction which brought $365,000 to the widow of Emerson McMillan, self-made financier. According to Henry Bischoff, Mahwah historian, furnishings included tapestries, rugs, bronzes, porcelains, period furniture and objects of art. Two years later the Diocese of Newark purchased the eleven hundred acre estate as a new site for its theological seminary. *Courtesy Newark Public Library*

174

Dedicatory exercises at the Ralph S. Maugham Elementary School in Tenafly honored the educator who had been involved in the educational, political and financial promotion of the borough since his arrival in 1886. Teacher, principal, superintendent of schools, borough petitioner, organist and choir master, Ralph Sylvester Maugham's career in Tenafly was typical of those exceptional men whose dedication to service enriched many a Bergen County community. He appears here, three years before his death in 1932, flanked by his grandchildren. Courtesy Virginia Mosley, Tenafly Borough Historian

Teaneck's handsome high school, located between Queen Anne and Teaneck roads, was built in 1929, immediately before Route 4 was constructed along the northern border of the property. As the town grew, the high school was enlarged in 1936, 1955 and again in 1976. The 1936 addition was constructed under one of the federal work projects generated by the Depression. Courtesy Newark Public Library

As is often the case, compulsory attendance at Bergen County schools was not always popular with the young. In this 1935 photograph, a Tenafly patrolman assists a reluctant scholar at the corner of George Street and West Clinton Avenue. Courtesy Virginia Mosley, Tenafly Borough Historian

In September 1942, Fairleigh Dickinson Junior College opened its doors in Rutherford to fifty-nine women and one man, the latter a not altogether unexpected result of initiating a college on the day following the Japanese attack on Pearl Harbor. Led for the greater part of forty years by Dr. Peter Sammartino, president and presently chancellor, the colleges of Fairleigh Dickinson University have expanded into three campuses, in Bergen County at Rutherford, Teaneck and Hackensack. Courtesy New Jersey Room, Fairleigh Dickinson University, Rutherford

As World War II called upon the youth of Bergen County, the Sheehans of Wood-Ridge faced the future with a grin. Aviation Cadet Schlenz of Wyckoff posed in his flight jacket and goggles. Courtesy The History of Wood-Ridge Committee and The News, Wyckoff

McGuire Air Force Base in southern New Jersey is named for Bergen County "ace" Thomas B. McGuire, Jr., shown here in the South Pacific in his P-38. The Ridgewood flier destroyed thirty-eight Japanese aircraft during the eighteen months prior to his fatal crash. He was killed while attempting to aid a fellow flier under attack. The second leading flying "ace" of World War II, his decorations included the Distinguished Service Cross, three Silver Stars, six Distinguished Flying Crosses and fifteen Air Medals. Twenty-four years old at the time of his death, Major McGuire was posthumously awarded the Congressional Medal of Honor. Courtesy 438th Military Airlift Wing, McGuire Air Force Base, NJ

Before the end of World War II, Wright Aeronautical Corporation, a division of Curtiss-Wright, had sent more than 10,000 aircraft engines to the West Coast for installation in Air Force B-29s. Their huge

Wood-Ridge plant was constructed in 1942 in a cabbage field purchased from Leopold Brandenburg who operated one of the few remaining farms in Wood-Ridge. Courtesy Newark Public Library

The nation's air raid warning system, adapted from the British experience, provided net-works of communication within each community. These Edgewater wardens were expected to patrol street blocks, enforce blackout and traffic regulations, and direct persons to shelters during an air alert. Their whistles signalled their whereabouts while on patrol. Courtesy Edgewater Public Library

Federal regulations required that air raid wardens complete two hours of military drill, conducted, in some communities, by the Military Police Reserve. Here Teaneck's wardens are put through their paces by drill masters in fedoras. Courtesy Teaneck Public Library

Bergen County suburbanites returned to the land, raising their own vegetables in "Victory Gardens," as the armed forces made heavy demands on the nation's food supply. At the formal opening of Wood-Ridge's Victory Garden in April 1943, two would-be farmers rake their plots on land donated by Madsen and Christensen, local florists. The New York City skyline appears in the haze on the horizon. Courtesy History of Wood-Ridge Committee

During World War II, money alone was not sufficient to purchase those commodities being rapidly devoured in great quantity by the American war machine. With the rest of the nation, Bergen County housewives learned to cope with ration stamps, a specialized form of currency issued by the Office of Price Administration (OPA). At regular intervals, each household was issued a ration book similar to the one illustrated here, and purchases of sugar, meat, butter and cheese were limited to the number of appropriate stamps remaining. Courtesy Harold Tallman, Cresskill Borough Historian

GASOLINE RATION CARD

WAR BONDS AND STAMPS

Nº 1016703 -A

THE ACCEPTANCE AND USE OF THIS CARD CONSTITUTE AN AGREEMENT THAT THE HOLDER WILL OBSERVE THE RULES AND REGULATIONS GOVERNING GASOLINE RATIONING AS ISSUED BY THE OFFICE OF PRICE ADMINISTRATION

OWNER'S NAME _John E. Hofmann_
STREET ADDRESS _John St._
CITY OR POST OFFICE _Demarest_ STATE _N. J._
MAKE _Chev_ BODY STYLE _Sedan_
VEHICLE REGISTRATION NO. _L 736_ STATE OF REGISTRATION _N. J._

READ INSTRUCTIONS ON REVERSE SIDE OF THIS CARD

Gasoline and tires were also rationed according to the owner's use of the family car. Drivers whose automobiles were not necessary to their employment or to the defense effort, were limited to an "A" sticker which allowed them only three gallons of gas per week. Courtesy Demarest Public Library

Although Tenafly's war bond drive, sponsored by the Lions Club, sold more than enough bonds to purchase a bomber, research has uncovered no evidence to suggest that the "Spirit of Tenafly" ever flew a mission. Courtesy Virginia Mosley, Tenafly Borough Historian

WANTED --

MORE SALVAGE TO SAVE LIVES!

Hundreds of Teaneck Public School Children have been enrolled in

A JUNIOR ARMY OF SALVAGE WARDENS

TO SOLICIT THE FULLEST COOPERATION OF ALL TEANECK RESIDENTS IN THE MOST IMPORTANT AND VITAL PHASE OF CIVILIAN WAR EFFORT

Principals, Teachers and Students of all Teaneck elementary schools have enlisted in a vast town-wide program designed to increase the flow of urgently needed salvage from the homes of the Township.

HOW YOU CAN HELP

SAVE WASTE PAPER

Waste paper is desperately needed to keep Bergen County paper mills in operation turning out bomb bands, powder and shell containers, aircraft parts, parachute flares, millions of K-ration boxes, blood plasma containers, and thousands of other paper products required by our fighting forces overseas in increasing quantities.

Tie all newspapers, magazines, books and other waste paper securely into convenient-size bundles. All loose paper, cracker boxes, envelopes, letters, circulars, etc., should be put into cartons or bags and securely tied.

Place on the curb before noon on Collection Day — THE FIRST SUNDAY OF EACH MONTH.

SAVE TIN CANS

Tin cans MUST be washed and flattened. It takes only a few minutes to remove the labels and to wash it clean of food. Every can counts. Save them in bags or boxes and put them out for curb pick-up on Collection Day.

SAVE RAGS

Save old clothing, cast-off garments, curtains, carpets, and articles of cotton, linen and wool. Tie rags into bundles or stuff into bags or boxes. Place on the curb with other material for salvage collection.

SAVE SCRAP METALS

Search your house for all old metal. If you don't need it, now is the time to put it to work for Uncle Sam. Place on the curb for collection.

SAVE WASTE FATS

Save at least a tablespoon of kitchen fats a day. Store in a clean can, kept cold. When you have a pound or more take it to your butcher. He will pay you for it and give you two red ration points for every pound you give him.

TEANECK VOLUNTEER SALVAGE WARDENS ARE ASKING FOR

A BUNDLE FROM EVERY HOME

NOTE THESE COLLECTION DATES:
THE FIRST SUNDAY OF EVERY MONTH
May 7, June 4, July 2, August 6
beginning at 12 noon.

TEANECK SALVAGE COMMITTEE
George E. Clayton, Director
MUNICIPAL BUILDING, TEANECK, N. J.

On the home front, Bergen County communities responded enthusiastically to the salvage drives which contributed tons of strategic materials to the war effort. Teaneck schoolchildren pulled their wagons from house to house collecting the paper, rags and metals which were in short supply. Courtesy Teaneck Public Library

Oradell's scrap metal pile included machine guns and German helmets from World War I. Courtesy Oradell Public Library

Honor rolls appeared in every Bergen County community, as they did nation-wide. Edgewater's tribute included three memorial crosses for men who did not return. Courtesy Edgewater Public Library

chapter 6

When the cloverleaf intersection of Routes 4 and 17 was designed in the early 1930s, engineers could not have forseen the volume of traffic which two busy shopping centers would generate twenty-five years in the future. First in the field, the Garden State Plaza, pictured above, attracted seventy-five thousand to opening day ceremonies, May 1, 1957. A subsidiary of R. H. Macy & Co., the shopping center covered 110 acres on opening day and provided parking space for fifty-five hundred cars. This early aerial view looks south along Route 17. A drive-in movie appears at right center. Courtesy Newark Public Library

A Good Place To Live

"Now is the time to look to the future and ask what sorts of places Teaneck and Hackensack and Bogota will be ten years from now. Will they be beautifully planned cities with streets for homes, streets for businesses, schools and playgrounds and parks; or will they be unlovely unplanned communities like too many of the over-crowded suburbs that have received Manhattan's overflow?"

This call to responsible community development was issued by a spokesman for the Regional Plan Association in 1931 as the George Washington Bridge was just being completed. The Great Depression effectively halted for a decade the growth that the bridge had promised, but the 1940s saw a dramatic change. The jobs and income generated by wartime contracts at plants such as Curtis Wright in Wood-Ridge were important, as was the tide of returning veterans, each looking for their dream home in the suburbs. Changes in banking and finance policies which came during the thirties were important also; changes which allowed for the longer term mortgages most working people required if they were to become homeowners. Bergen underwent a veritable explosion of development and was soon on its way to becoming the most populous county in the state.

The new press of development brought with it row after row of tract houses—Cape Cods and split levels by the thousands. In built up areas garden apartment complexes became more common, some of them "Veterans' Emergency Homes," built in part with state funding and intended especially for returning GIs and their families. In established neighborhoods where there was no room for further building, single family homes were occasionally pressed into extra service as attics and basements were transformed into cramped little apartments.

The millions of Americans who set their sights on a new life in the suburbs in the post World War II era were driven by a variety of motives. The two most common were a desire for the fresh air and open space available outside the city, and the opportunity to settle in a community of people of similar wealth, status and social values. In this sense, the new suburbanites exhibited the trends which sociologist David Riesman identified in the contemporary culture. According to Riesman, America had reached a new plateau of psycho-social development

in which traditional and "inner-directed" patterns of social life were being set aside in exchange for a new "other-directedness." Most people, he argued, were now willing to base their self image, their social status and even their sense of morality on what was acceptable to the people around them. What was popularly called "keeping up with the Joneses," represented a perceived need for people to be, first and foremost, "well-adjusted"—they had to "fit in."

Riesman's ideas merged perfectly with those of many intellectuals of the period who criticized what they saw as a sterile and insulated lifestyle common to the suburbs. Lewis Mumford attacked the suburb as "a segregated community, set aside from the city, not merely by space, but by class stratification: a sort of green ghetto dedicated to the elite." Set apart from the problems of society that had been left behind in the cities, people sought "the whole meaning of life in the most elemental social group, the family, or even in the more isolated and self-centered individual." The end product, Mumford explained, would be "an encapsulated life spent more and more either in the motor car or within the cabin of darkness before the television set." Here was the fulfillment of Riesman's *Lonely Crowd*.

Quite a different opinion was expressed by the United States government when, in 1949, the army singled out Bergen's Teaneck from among ten thousand American towns as the model community with which to illustrate to the occupied nations of Europe and Asia the benefits of American democracy in action. As the *New York Times* put it, Teaneck showed the world "how a small city government is organized, how it functions and how such a system can provide for the varied needs of community life."

In the 1930s Teaneck had provided a model for regulating building and development. Neighborhood zoning, one of the tools they used successfully, had been introduced by planners in the '20s to regulate the haphazard development of commercial strips along highways. In the years after World War II, rapid development led to broader applications of such techniques. By the end of the 1950s, the chairman of the Bergen County Planning Board could proclaim that every one of Bergen's seventy communities was regulating development with such zoning ordinances.

On the surface zoning codes were intended to

One of the first concerns of Bergen County's returned G.I. was to find a house or apartment for himself and his family. The dearth of residential construction during the previous fifteen years, combined with the depreciation of already aging buildings resulted in an acute shortage in the housing market. Many new families were at a loss, especially those generated by war-time marriages. Municipalities all over the county experimented with a variety of solutions. Pictured here is one of Teaneck's veterans' apartment complexes erected in 1947 with state and township funds. By 1951 Teaneck had housed 130 veterans' families in three developments. *Courtesy Teaneck Public Library*

Many veterans would have considered themselves fortunate to locate a compact attic apartment in a single family house such as the one pictured here in Hackensack circa 1941. *Courtesy Paterson Museum*

protect and preserve established community values, but they also represented the modern suburbanites' desire to disassociate themselves from the problems of the cities and of neighboring communities. Whereas some communities had formally established restrictive covenants which forbade sale to Negroes or other minorities, informal methods were no less effective. The historians of Mahwah note that for decades the residents of the Cragmere community upheld the unwritten rule "don't sell to a Jew." By limiting the minimum size of a building plot or the square footage of dwellings to be built, municipal zoning ordinances could just as effectively keep out the poor and others regarded as undesirables. Where minority populations already existed, zoning became a tool of segregation, strictly defining the neighborhoods in which apartment houses and other multiple dwellings were permitted. Typically, moving out had also meant moving up. The suburbanites' characteristic response was "why should it be my responsibility?" For many communities in Bergen County and elsewhere in the nation, zoning laws became the last line of defense against intrusion by unwanted problems—both environmental and human problems—which suburban dwellers had tried to escape in the first place.

At about the same time as the designers of Radburn had begun to lay out their "motor age" city, another developer, Jesse C. Nichols, was planning his suburban sub-divisions on the outskirts of Kansas City. But Nichols took his provisions for the automobile a step further; his residential district would also have a "shopping plaza," a concentration of quality stores with plentiful off-street parking located at a hub of suburban traffic flow. Nichols is credited with inventing the concept of the "suburban mall," examples of which sprouted up all over America after World War II.

When shopping center developers turned to New

One lucky veteran was surprised to learn that his one dollar bid had won a six-room house offered at auction by the Teaneck Town Council. The Army Air Force veteran had been house-hunting for eight months following his military discharge. In the photograph he happily points to his new home as he waves the dollar he owes the Township of Teaneck. Courtesy Newark Public Library

Jersey they found a retailers' dreamland in Bergen County. Of the more than three thousand counties in the United States, Bergen ranked twentieth in per capita income, yet most of that money was spent outside the county in places like Paterson, Newark and New York City. Population was booming in the area, a population of young and prosperous families anxious to consume. Moreover, plans for the improvement of Routes 4 and 17, the completion of the Garden State Parkway through Bergen, and the construction of the lower level of the George Washington Bridge, would put over 1.5 million people within a forty minute drive of the little town of Paramus where the highways intersected. National attention turned to the place where, for the first time, two major regional shopping centers were to be built within three-quarters of a mile of one another. An article in the journal *Traffic Quarterly* argued that:

With the establishment of the two huge regional centers, it is likely that the poles of the magnet will be reversed, and that the area will not only retain the major part of its own large purchasing power, but will draw off a considerable amount of business from the older traffic congested cities surrounding it, including New York.

When the Garden State Plaza and the Bergen Mall opened their doors (and their parking lots) in 1957, they created in the heart of Bergen County the largest suburban shopping complex in the country.

The 1960s and 1970s saw continuing transition. While both population and development continued to expand for most of the period, some of the symbols of earlier vitality were disappearing. The railroads which had provided the life's blood of the nineteenth and early twentieth century suburbs, sharply cut back operations reflecting changing patterns of where people worked and how they got there. Palisades Park closed its gates for the last time in 1971, sold to a developer who was planning to build a string of high-rise luxury buildings along the river. While some of the better established downtown commercial centers continued to prosper (Ridgewood and Englewood are good examples), others suffered in competition with the multiplying shopping centers and highway stores.

One of the changes in work patterns in America at this time was the increase in white collar jobs, which surpassed blue collar jobs nationwide for the first time in 1956. This larger shift was reflected in the growing number of companies which chose Bergen County as the location for their corporate headquarters. In dramatic illustration of continuing blue collar decline, Bergen's largest single industrial plant, the huge Ford assembly plant in Mahwah ceased operations in 1980. Finding ways to retrain and reemploy those workers displaced by the closing of the Mahwah plant as well as other victims of the shifting economy will continue to present problems.

Resources for education and intellectual development expanded significantly during these years. Bergen communities had always been attentive to the need for quality schools. This had been one of the drives toward the establishment of so many independent municipalities in the county in the 1890s. The new suburbanites were even more mindful of the need for sound education. As children in city schools came to be described more and more often as "disadvantaged," Bergen County's children by contrast were surely "advantaged." Now there were colleges as well. Fairleigh Dickinson University, Bergen Community College and Ramapo College have each contributed to the county's cultural capital and provided significant amenities for the public at large. Many of the newcomers who were

Hackensack Gardens.
Ralph Carletta & Charles Rocco, Builders.
Maniscalco & Hecker, Architects.

Increased demand for housing led to the proliferation of new garden apartments, two or three story units clustered around central courts. Hackensack Gardens, built in 1948 in the block below Essex Street and Summit Avenue in Hackensack offered three and four- room units which rented for seventy and eighty dollars per month. Courtesy Newark Public Library

history learned about it during the Bicentennial of the American Revolution celebrated in 1976. The re-enactment of Washington's dramatic retreat from the British at Fort Lee was extended across the State. In addition, Bergen had a front row seat for what was one of the nation's foremost Bicentennial events—the parade of the tall ships up the Hudson.

At three hundred years of age, Bergen faces new challenges and new opportunities. In many ways suburban life is no longer what it used to be. Suburbanites who twenty-five years ago bought their little piece of Bergen County so that they could enjoy the open spaces and reside among people just like themselves, now live with a population density becoming progressively urbanized and with far more cosmopolitan racial and ethnic mix. In 1965, as described in Reginald G. Damerell's book, *Triumph in a White Suburb*, Teaneck addressed the problem of racial prejudice and became the first community in the nation to vote for the voluntary integration of its schools. More recently the concentration of Japanese in the Fort Lee area has led one journalist to refer to it as "Nippon on the Hudson." Older closed communities may prefer to stay the way they are, but even the settlements of the "mountain people" or "Jackson Whites" nestled in the Ramapos face a challenge that seems irresistable.

Other forces which threaten to blur further the distinctions between the city and suburb include recent challenges to restrictive zoning laws. In Mahwah, for example, the community zoning ordinance was challenged in the courts for failing to allow for dwellings affordable to people such as those who worked in that town's industrial plants. The closing of the Ford factory muted the point, but the argument remains in Mahwah and elsewhere. Another issue involves the New Jersey Supreme Court's decision regarding the funding of public education and guaranteeing that the constitutional rights of children to a quality education should not depend upon the affluence of their particular community. New Jersey now leads other states in seeking to balance expenditures for schools in richer and poorer districts.

Still other pressures challenge the independence of Bergen's seventy municipalities. As problems have become more complex and less amenable to local solutions, towns have been forced to sacrifice autonomy in certain areas. In response to a 1968 state law establishing the Hackensack Meadowlands Development Commission (HMDC), Bergen communities (with others from neighboring Hudson County) were forced to turn over authority to regulate development in the Meadowlands District. A decade later perhaps the most significant achievement of the HMDC has been the limitation of open garbage dumping from communities all over Northern New Jersey. Recently, in an effort to deal more effectively with that dumping which continues, they have installed the world's largest trash compactor which packs the garbage into firm bundles. Then these become the building blocks for a new sculptured landscape destined eventually to be an inviting park. The future park's environment center, a strikingly modern building nestled next to a still growing mountain of garbage, opened in 1982. Environmentalists may disagree about the overall effectiveness of various Meadowlands development projects, but one thing is clear: these are problems which individual communities have never been able to address on their own.

All in all, efforts at planning the development of residential and industrial areas have resulted in a continued pleasant atmosphere for living. But Bergen County today shows shifting patterns which are common to larger suburban America. As elsewhere, for example, there are different types of suburban communities. Scholars have identified four characteristic types: exclusive upper-income suburbs, middle-class family suburbs, lower income work-

Real estate developers continued to exploit the post-war demand for housing. In 1952, a billboard on Route 17 advertised single-family homes in Ramsey for $16,990. Courtesy Paterson Museum

ing-class suburbs, and cosmopolite suburbs (places such as suburban college towns which appeal to artists and intellectuals). One might identify variations of all four types in Bergen County, New Jersey. It is also common these days across America, for fewer suburbanites to commute to the city for work, shopping or leisure. When the *New York Times* reported the results of a "suburban poll" it had taken in 1978 it noted that "the residents of the ring around New York City, once regarded simply as a bedroom for commuters, no longer feel themselves subordinate to New York." Most admitted to going to the city infrequently if at all, and 54 percent even declined to think of themselves as part of the greater metropolitan area. As Peter O. Muller explains in a recent article in *American Quarterly*, metropolitan America is becoming a sort of mosaic, fragmented into a series of "multi-purpose suburban downtowns or 'mini cities,' which can already provide a full array of urban goods and services to their local surrounding population."

That population today defies the easy characterizations that may have been possible several decades ago. The typical family with 2.3 children has given way to all sorts of alternative living arrangements. More of the unmarried or older people who in earlier eras may have been more likely to prefer city life, today live in the suburbs. Indeed, many apartment complexes and condominium developments today cater to singles or childless couples; and bars, discos and health clubs along the highways try to attract the "unattached." As housing prices, mortgage rates and real estate taxes soar, some retired people on fixed incomes are unable to stay in the homes in which they raised their families, and many young people who grew up in the area find it financially impossible to bring their wives and children back to live in their own suburban dream homes. Such economic pressures may serve as effectively to retain segregation by income group as any pattern of restrictive zoning.

Today the shopping mall is the place where people most often come together. For many, it is a place of entertainment where they can have dinner, see a film, browse and watch people. For vast numbers of Bergen teenagers, like their counterparts in southern California and elsewhere across America, the mall is a place to meet and "hang out." It has been predicted that shopping centers in the eighties will become America's new community centers, duplicating all of the social and cultural functions of the traditional "Main Street." In Bergen the situation is complicated further by the proliferation of centers, many of them through their careful selection of stores appealing to one class of consumers over another.

Surely suburbia still has critics. Life there, as everywhere, is less than perfect. We have learned that environmental pollution and social problems such as drug abuse can occur anywhere. One hopes that those who persist in pointing out the flaws of life in our "green ghettoes," as Mumford called them, might learn from some of the mistaken judgments made before. The tendency, for example, to blame suburbia for problems related to racial prejudice or the growing dominance of the mass media, stemmed from a simple failure to see how deeply rooted these forces were in the entire culture. Perhaps those who castigate life in the suburbs as sterile and unfulfilling, would do well to consider the alternatives for most people who, after all, were doing their best to improve their own lives and those of their families. All is not perfect in year 300, but Bergen continues to be one of the nation's very richest counties in cultural and historical as well as in financial terms. Millions of Americans wish that they could live as well.

Apartment house living in Bergen County reached its apogee with the appearance of high-rise apartment clusters atop the Palisades from Fort Lee to Edgewater. Attracted by the spectacular views and convenient location, many transplanted New Yorkers now enjoy the relatively slower pace of Bergen County communities. The sixth unit of the Horizon House complex pictured here was completed in 1967, and offered a housing mix from studio to three-room apartments renting from $200 to $625 per month. Courtesy Newark Public Library

These photographs of Teaneck teen-agers traveled to Japan, the Ryukyu Islands, and Austria after World War II in an exhibit of thirty pictures mounted by the U.S. Army to demonstrate American democratic processes and community life to United States-occupied countries. Photographers spent three days in September 1949 documenting activities in the township after the Army's Civil Affairs Division chose Teaneck from a field of ten thousand as a model American community. The young people pictured here are enjoying themselves at Teaneck Town House, a popular gathering spot for all ages operated by the township's Recreation Department. Courtesy Teaneck Public Library

Most shoppers are unaware of the busy traffic beneath their feet as merchandise moves in and out of the Garden State Plaza through loading bays connected to underground truck tunnels. Courtesy Newark Public Library

In 1957 Bergen County's shopping horizons were widened further by the opening of a second complex, The Bergen Mall, barely one mile east of the Garden State Plaza on Route 4. Designed by John Graham of New York and Seattle, the mall was built by Allied Stores Corporation at a cost of forty million dollars. TV personality, Dave Garroway served as Master of Ceremonies on opening day, November 14, following his popular "Today" show, televised from the spot. James O'Grady, the mall's general manager pictured above, welcomed the opening day crowd. Courtesy Seymour Malkin

Whether by accident or by design, the large shopping malls came to serve as centers of popular culture as well. At Bergen Mall's popular "Music on the Mall" summer concerts, listeners provided their own lawn chairs. The concert pictured above featured the Waldwick Band, conducted by Dr. Walter E. Nallin, a Waldwick resident and Professor of Music at City College of New York. Courtesy Seymour Malkin

Nike-Ajax missiles are unloaded at Mahwah Station for the trip to launching pads in the Ramapo Mountains. Mahwah's missile base was located in the Fardale section, just off Campgaw Road near the Immaculate Conception Seminary. Begun in June 1954, there were twelve launching pads in operation by 1958, each holding a one-ton missile designed to intercept intercontinental ballistic missiles aimed at the metropolitan area. The base was closed in the early 1960s in a reorganization which placed greater emphasis on Nike-Hercules units. Some of the buildings were used by Ramapo College before its main campus was completed in 1971. Courtesy The News, *Wyckoff*

Workmen constructed a model atomic bomb shelter in Ridgewood's East Ridgewood Avenue Plaza in 1959. Contractor John King of Midland Park estimated the cost of a home shelter at $400; $175 for the home handyman. Courtesy The Ridgewood NEWSpapers

School children in Wyckoff take shelter beneath their desks during an air-raid alert in the 1950s. Richard Butler Turner photograph. Courtesy The News, *Wyckoff*

Garments on this Oakland clothesline received an extra rinse from the Ramapo River in August of 1955 after hurricanes Connie and Diane dumped more than eleven inches of water on Bergen County in little more than a week. With the river rising at the rate of once inch per hour, Civil Defense personnel were alerted at 3:00 AM on August 19 to assist in the evacuation of 100 homes, many of them summer bungalows.

Displaced Oakland residents and vacationers took refuge in the Ponds Memorial Building. Courtesy The News, Wyckoff

Until the introduction of the Salk vaccine in 1951, concerned parents followed the reported incidence of infantile paralysis, a crippling disease active particularly among young school children during late summer and early fall. In 1954 Bergen was one of five counties chosen by the New Jersey State Commissioner of Health to participate in a nation-wide program of voluntary innoculation of second grade students. By 1956 the vaccine was available to everyone, and the disease declined dramatically. The Wyckoff schoolboy pictured above faced the ordeal of his "shot" with a grin, or perhaps mixed emotions. Richard Butler Turner photograph. Courtesy The News, Wyckoff

Little League founder Carl Stotz was firmly committed to the concept that every boy should have an opportunity to play baseball. From a modest beginning in Williamsport, Pennsylvania in the late 1930s, baseball teams for boys eight to twelve years old appeared in communities all over the United States, gaining particular impetus after World War II. Pictured here, flashing victory grins, are the players who won first place in Englewood's National League in 1953. In the 1970s, girls became eligible for Englewood teams, and in 1983 the Little League president was a woman. *Courtesy Englewood Public Library*

During the 1950s, boys from eleven to fifteen years of age competed for a place in the national Soap Box Derby held each August in Akron, Ohio, where the top prize was a fifteen thousand-dollar college scholarship, full four-year tuition in those days to the college of one's choice. Young drivers were often sponsored by clubs or business organizations, but the rules stipulated that the racers be built by the boys themselves at a cost not to exceed $10. Although the designs of the Wyckoff racers pictured here vary widely, their builders have obviously observed the $10 rule. *Courtesy* The News, *Wyckoff*

Bingo was an adult recreation which flourished as churches and other organizations realized the game's fund-raising potential. At this game sponsored by Mount Virgin Church in Garfield, the men in aprons patrolling the aisles, furnished the players with cards and change. On the stage, officials call out the numbers which must appear in sequence on straight or diagonal lines on the cards to qualify for the lucky BINGO. *Courtesy Newark Public Library*

Bergen County has more than four times as many people per square mile than are found in Japan. The county's population doubled between 1930 and 1960, and thereafter continued to grow until the 1980 census recorded the county's first population loss in 300 years. New Jersey's fourth most densely populated county, in 1970 Bergen accommodated 3,824.6 persons in 234.57 square miles. The photograph dramatically highlights the housing clustered around Bergen's busy hub at the intersection of Routes 17 and 4 in Paramus. Courtesy Public Service Electric and Gas Company

As Bergen County began to offer more sophisticated opportunities for merchandizing, recreation and cultural events, fewer residents found it necessary or desirable to travel to New York City. The county's railroads, already ambivalent concerning commuter traffic, concentrated instead upon the more profitable freight trains, consigning many of their erstwhile passengers to buses and car pools. As the passenger trains disappeared, commercial ventures pre-empted local depots, exploiting their central locations and Victorian charm. When this photograph was taken in 1966, the Erie Station on Engle Street in Englewood had been converted into a women's clothing shop. Courtesy Newark Public Library restaurant. Courtesy Newark Public Library

The first automobile rolls off Ford Motor's assembly line in the new plant in Mahwah. The largest automobile assembly unit in the United States when it opened in 1955, the facility's floor space covered almost two million square feet, with a conveyor network ten miles long. One thousand cars per day were driven off the assembly line during the plant's peak production years in the 1960s and 1970s. Courtesy The Ridgewood NEWSpapers

Twenty-five years later Mahwah officials reacted with shock and disbelief as the company moved to close the plant in the summer of 1980, adding thirty-eight hundred workers to the ranks of the unemployed. During the Mahwah years, Ford workers produced over 4.5 million automobiles and more than 1.3 million trucks. Here a United Automobile Workers official poses in the last car off the line, June 20, 1980 rolling past a displaced employee whose T-shirt offers satirical advice to a celebrated Georgia peanut farmer. Star-Ledger photograph, courtesy Newark Public Library

The postwar years found automobiles in short supply with a seller's market in both new and used cars. Little Ferry was the acknowledged used car center for northern New Jersey with twelve dealers operating lots along Route 6 (now 46) in 1947. This photograph was taken in 1949 after the used-car trade had hit its peak. Courtesy Newark Public Library

Not many Bergenites today would be able to identify the Bergen-Passaic Expressway although the name was often in the news when the limited access highway was under construction in the early 1960s. The expressway became the easternmost section of Interstate Route 80, that important artery which crosses the entire country from San Francisco to the George Washington Bridge. All local lanes and connecting ramps from the bridge to the Garden State Parkway were opened in December 1964. The photograph shows road crews at work in October of that year near the concrete arch connecting Leonia and Englewood in what is now a section of Interstate Route 95. Courtesy Newark Public Library

Confronted with escalating rents and taxes in New York City, many prominent corporations looked to Bergen County for a new location convenient to the metropolitan area. An aerial view of Englewood Cliffs shows some of the corporate headquarters along Route 9W, one of three roads leading to the George Washington Bridge. Courtesy Public Service Electric and Gas Company

Following World War II, Bergen County continued to supply local and metropolitan markets with fresh farm produce, albeit grown on consistently declining acreage. In 1948 sweet corn occupied first place in the county's acreage, followed by tomatoes, cabbage, spinach and celery. This 1947 photograph of productive land in Paramus was taken from East Ridgewood Avenue. The area has since been commercially developed. Courtesy Newark Public Library

Although the employment of migrant farm workers is most often associated with southern New Jersey, in 1960 there were forty-eight such camps in Bergen County, housing Puerto Ricans, black Americans and British West Indians. Small camps predominated with only five farmers employing more than eight workers. Here two migrants paint their new quarters at a Mahwah farm after their previous lodgings had been condemned by state inspectors. At the time of this photograph in 1959, farm workers averaged eighty cents per hour in the area. Courtesy The Ridgewood NEWSpapers

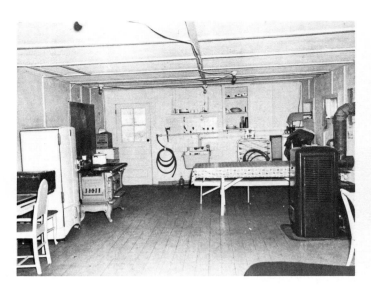

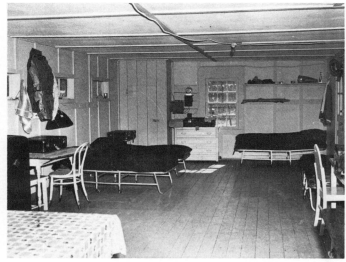

Most of the migrant housing in the county was equipped with running water, stove and refrigerator. However, in 1960, only one quarter of the units had been provided with flush toilets, and fewer than that with hot water. The Puerto Rican women who occupied the quarters above were supplied with all the amenities except for shower and toilet facilities which were located in the barn. Employed by a Wyckoff nursery, five or six women returned annually during the growing season. Courtesy The Ridgewood NEWSpapers

A view of Bergen Community College's "E" Building, the site of the college's modest beginnings in the late 1960s. Located on an 167 acre campus in Paramus, the county's first public two-year college offers programs leading to an Associate of Arts degree. Founded in 1965 by the Bergen County Board of Chosen Freeholders, the college's first class attracted 1,454 students in 1968, a figure which would grow to nearly 12,000 by 1982. Courtesy Bergen Community College

Ramapo College students stroll beneath the Havemeyer Arch which guards the driveway to the college's administration building, a mansion built by Theodore Havemeyer in the late 1880s for his married daughter, Natalie Mayer. Trustees of the proposed State College of Northern New Jersey bought three hundred acres of the Stephen Birch estate in 1970. Conceived as an alternative to existing four-year colleges, the new liberal arts institution was committed to an unconventional educational structure and to innovative programs designed to attract a heterogeneous mix of students. After a change of name in 1970, Ramapo College opened in 1971 and graduated its first class four years later. The windowed structure to the right is one of the academic buildings which have won numerous awards for architectural excellence. Courtesy The Ridgewood NEWSpapers

Contemporary architecture provides walkways and vistas for the spacious campus, formerly the Orchard Hills Country Club. Perched two stories in the air, the Administrative Section of Bergen Community's main building presents an imposing facade. Courtesy Bergen Community College

Walter M. Schirra, Bergen County's first man in space, is shown here with a model of the Project Mercury spacecraft which he piloted in six orbits 175 miles above the earth in 1962. Born in Hackensack in 1923, "Wally" Schirra attended primary and junior high school in Oradell, and was graduated from Dwight Morrow High School in Englewood. After his graduation from the United States Naval Academy in 1945, Schirra flew ninety combat missions in Korea for which he won two Air Medals and the Distinguished Flying Cross. One of the first seven astronauts chosen by NASA in 1959, Schirra also piloted the Gemini 6 flight of 1965. His last venture into space was as commander of Apollo 7 in an eleven-day test of the spacecraft which later took Americans to the moon. Courtesy National Aeronautics and Space Administration

Grim reminder of the U.S. Atlantic Fleet which patrolled our shores during the anxious days of World War II, the U.S.S. Ling now lies moored in the Hackensack River at the foot of Borg Park on River Street in Hackensack. In December 1971, the submarine was decommissioned and donated to the Submarine Memorial Association, a group of former submariners and other interested citizens

dedicated to the preservation of this submarine. Members of the association prepared the dock site and raised funds to renovate the undersea vessel. Since January 1975 this unique museum has played host to Bergen County schoolchildren and to other assorted groups, as well as to the occasional passer-by. Courtesy Submarine Memorial Association

During the Bicentennial of the United States in 1976, Bergen County, its municipalities and related institutions, celebrated the nation's 200th birthday in a series of programs inspired by the creativity of involved citizens. Bergen County locations provided unparalled views of one of the most spectacular national celebrations, Operation Sail, reminiscent of the return of the Santiago Fleet at the turn of the century. Led by the Coast Guard training ship, Eagle, 212 tall ships from thirty-four nations sailed majestically up the Hudson River to the George Washington Bridge where they turned for the return trip down the river. Apartment dwellers in high-rises along the Bergen County Palisades did not lack for guests on that Fourth of July. Notice the "76" motif in the flower bed. Courtesy The Record, Hackensack

The Hackensack Meadowlands Development Commission was created in 1968 with a mandate from the New Jersey Legislature to oversee the orderly development of the Hackensack Meadows, a region which includes parts of fourteen municipalities in Bergen and Hudson counties. The commission's master plan provides for the creation of jobs, housing, recreation and open space, while maintaining the area's delicate ecological balance. The commission's Environment and Visitors Center pictured here serves as the focal point for the expanded educational, recreational and economic programs planned by the HMDC. Located in the Lyndhurst meadows, the new facility also serves as the Commission's headquarters. *Courtesy New Jersey Newsphotos*

The best seat in the house—a raft in the river just off Edgewater. Courtesy **The Record,** *Hackensack*

Bibliography

"Additional Notes on the Cherry Hill Tornado." *Bergen County History* (1973), 57-58.

Aviation Hall of Fame of New Jersey: Preserving a Distinguished Aeronautical Heritage. [Teterboro, N. J.]: Aviation Hall of Fame, [1981?].

Bailey, Anthony. "Radburn Revisited." *Regional Plan News*, 76 (Dec. 1964), 1-5.

Bailey, Rosalie Fellows. *Pre-Revolutionary Dutch Houses and Families in Northern New Jersey and Southern New York.* New York: William Morrow, 1936.

Barber, John W. and Howe, Henry. *Historical Collections of the State of New Jersey.* New York: S. Tuttle, 1845.

Bassett, William B. *Historic American Buildings Survey of New Jersey.* Compiled and edited for the Historic American Buildings Survey....Ed. by John Poppeliers. Newark, N.J., The New Jersey Historical Society, 1977.

Beers, F. W. *Atlas of the Hudson River Valley from New York City to Troy.* New York: Watson & Co., 1891.

Bergen County Historical Society. "Report of the Committee on Current History." *Annual Report, Bergen County Historical Society*, 15 (1921-22), 88-89.

Bergen County Police Department. *30th Anniversary Ball.* [Hackensack, N.J.]: The Department, 1950.

Bergen County Superintendent of Schools. *Superintendent's Annual Circular of Greeting to the Graduates of Bergen County, New Jersey. Class of 1900.* [Hackensack, N.J.], 1900.

Bird, Eugene K. *Windjammers of the Hackensack.* Hackensack, N.J.: The Hackensack Republican, [1916?].

Bischoff, Henry and Kahn, Mitchell. *From Pioneer Settlement to Suburb: A History of Mahwah, New Jersey, 1700-1976.* South Brunswick, N.J.: A. S. Barnes, 1979.

Blauvelt, Hiram B. D., ed. *History of Oradell.* Oradell, N.J.: Borough of Oradell, [1944].

Bogert, Frederick W. *Paramus: A Chronicle of Four Centuries.* Paramus, N.J.: Paramus Free Public Library, 1961.

Bolton, Charles Knowles. *The Founders: Persons Born Abroad Who Came to the Colonies in North America Before the Year 1701.* [Boston]: The Boston Athenaeum, 1919. Vol. 1.

Boorstin, Daniel J. *The Americans: The Democratic Experience.* New York: Random House, 1973.

Boyd, John T. "Some Early Dutch Houses in New Jersey." *Architectural Record*, 36 (1914), 31-48.

Camp Merritt, New Jersey: September 1917-January 1920. [1924?].

"The Cherry Hill Tornado." *Bergen County History* (1972), 71-79.

Clark, Watson G. "The Location of Camp Merritt at Tenafly, N.J." *Eighteenth Annual Report of the Bergen County Historical Society*, 13 (1920), 55-58.

Clayton, W. Wood. *History of Bergen and Passaic Counties, New Jersey, With Biographical Sketches of Many of its Pioneers and Prominent Men.* Philadelphia: Everts and Peck, 1882.

Coffin, C. W. Floyd. "Bergen County: Planned Industrial Giant," *New Jersey Business* (June, 1960), 28-29.

Conniff, James C. G. and Conniff, Richard. *The Energy People.* Newark, N.J.: Public Service Electric and Gas Company, 1978.

Cooley, Henry Schofield. *A Study of Slavery in New Jersey:* Johns Hopkins University Studies in Historical and Political Science, 14th Series, 9-10, ed. Herbert B. Adams. Baltimore, 1896.

Cresskill, New Jersey Tercentenary Celebration, 1664-1964. Cresskill, N.J.: Tercentenary Committee, 1964.

Crump, J. Irving. *Oradell: Biography of a Borough.* Oradell, N.J.: Borough of Oradell, 1969.

Cunningham, John C. *New Jersey: A Mirror on America.* Florham Park, N.J.: Afton, 1978.

Damerell, Reginald. *Triumph in a White Suburb.* New York: William Morrow, 1968.

Demarest Civic Association. *A Map Showing Streets, Parks, Public Buildings, and Places of Interest in the Town in Which You Live.* Demarest, N.J.: The Association, 1952.

Derry, Ellis L. *Old and Historic Churches of New Jersey.* Union City, N.J.: Wm. H. Wise, 1979.

Directory of Hackensack and All Stations on the New Jersey and New York RR, 1896/97. Newburgh, N.Y.: Breed Publishing Co. [1896?].

Directory of Hackensack, Bogota, North Hackensack and Maywood (Bergen County, N.J.). Yonkers, N.Y.: W. L. Richmond, 1921/22.

Dolce, Phillip, ed. *Suburbia: The American Dream and Dilemma.* New York: Anchor Books, 1976.

Du Bois, Kathryn Phillips. *Old Mills of Bergen County: Histories and Family Records, 1677-1954.* [n.p.]: Phillips, [1954]. 2 vols. Typescript.

Durie, Howard I. *The Kakiat Patent in Bergen County, New Jersey: With Genealogical Accounts of Some of its Fifteen Early Settlers.* [Woodcliff Lake, N.J.: Durie], 1970.

Embry, Aymar. *Early American Churches.* Garden City, N.Y.: Doubleday, 1914.

The Fabric of History: A Commemorative History of Hasbrouck Heights, New Jersey. Hasbrouck Heights: Legislative and Civics Department, Junior Women's Club of Hasbrouck Heights, N.J., [1964].

Fort Lee, Past and Present. [Fort Lee, N.J.]: Fort Lee Chamber of Commerce, [1975?].

Gamble, Robert H. ed. *A Story of Industrial Progress: Bergen County Industrial Exposition.* [Hackensack, N.J.]: Bergen County Chamber of Commerce, 1953.

Goodman, Jack, ed. *While You Were Gone: A Report on Wartime Life in The United States.* New York: Simon and Schuster, 1946.

Greco, James J. *The Story of Englewood Cliffs.* Englewood Cliffs, N.J.: Tercentenary Committee, 1964.

Haberly, Loyd. *Newspapers and Newspapermen of Rutherford.* [Rutherford, N.J.]: published jointly by the Rutherford Committee on the New Jersey Tercentenary and Fairleigh Dickinson University, [1964?]

"Hackensack and New York Railroad Company." In *Annual Reports of the Railroad And Canal Companies of the State of New Jersey for the Year 1861.* Jersey City: printed by John H. Lyon, 1862.

Hackensack Meadowlands Development Commission. *A Report from the Hackensack Meadowlands Development Commission.* East Rutherford, N.J.: the Commission, 1981.

_____. Lyndhurst, N.J., 1982.

Hands, James A. "A Brief History of Rutherford, New Jersey." *Historical Program, Rutherford Diamond Jubilee, 1881-1956.* [Rutherford, N.J.: Diamond Jubilee Committee, 1956].

Harvey, Cornelius Burnham, ed. *Genealogical History of Hudson and Bergen Counties, New Jersey.* New York Genealogical Publishing Co., 1900.

Heusser, Albert H. *The History of the Silk Dyeing Industry in the United States.* Paterson, N.J.: Silk Dyers Assoc. of America, 1927.

History of Wood-Ridge Committee. *A History of Wood-Ridge.* [Wood-Ridge, N.J.]: Borough of Wood-Ridge, 1964.

"The Hudson River." *Art Journal,* n.s., Vol. 1 (1875), 41-44.

Hudson, Robert B. *Radburn, A Plan for Living: A Study Made for the American Association for Adult Education.* New York: The Association, 1934.

Humphrey, J.A. *Englewood: Its Annals and Reminiscences.* New York: J. S. Ogilvie Pub. Co., 1899.

Hussey, E. C., *Home Building.* 1876: Reprint. *Victorian Home Building.* Watkins Glen, N.Y.: The American Life Foundation, 1976.

Improved Order of Red Men. Great Council of New Jersey. *Records, Sixty-first Great Sun Session, 7th and 8th Suns, Worm Moon, G.S.D. 421, Trenton, New Jersey.* Camden, N.J.: C. S. Magrath, Printer, 1912.

Industries of New Jersey: Part IV: Hudson, Passaic, and Bergen Counties. New York: Historical Publishing Co. 1883.

Jackson, Martin H. *Hasbrouck Heights and the World War.* [Hasbrouck Heights, N.J.]: Business Men's Association, [1919?].

Johnson, William M. "Bergen County Courts." *Papers and Proceedings of the Bergen County Historical Society,* 7 (1910-1911), 9-20.

Kasson, John. *Amusing the Million: Coney Island at the Turn of the Century.* New York: Hill & Wang, 1978.

Keasbey, A. Q. "Slavery in New Jersey." *Proceedings of the New Jersey Historical Society.* 3rd. series. 4 (1901/05), 90-96, 147-154; 5 (1906/07), 12-20, 79-86.

Keesey, Ruth M. "Rivers and Roads in Old Bergen County." *De Halve Maen,* 39, nos. 3 & 4 (1965) and 40, nos. 1 & 2 (1965).

Ketchum, J. J., Morris, J. F., Mahoney, D. W. *Rutherford, New Jersey . . . : An Ideal Suburb.* [Rutherford, N.J.]: The Rutherford News, 1892.

Kirkbride's New Jersey Business Directory. Trenton: Stacy B. Kirkbride, 1850.

League of Women Voters of Teaneck, New Jersey. *Our Teaneck Schools.* Teaneck, New Jersey: The League, 1978.

Leaming, Aaron and Spicer, Jacob. *The Grants, Concessions and Original Constitutions of the Province of New Jersey.* Philadelphia: W. Bradford, [1751/2].

Leiby, Adrian C. *The Early Dutch and Swedish Settlers of New Jersey.* Princeton: D. Van Nostrand, 1964.

_____. *The Huguenot Settlement of Schraalenburgh: The History of Bergenfield, New Jersey.* Bergenfield, N.J.: Bergenfield Public Library, 1964.

_____. *The Revolutionary War in the Hackensack Valley: The Jersey Dutch and The Neutral Ground, 1775-1783.* New Brunswick, N.J.: Rutgers Univ. Press, 1963.

_____. *The United Churches of Hackensack and Schraalenburgh New Jersey, 1686-1822.* River Edge, N.J.: Bergen County Historical Society, 1976.

Leighton, Marshall Ora. *Passaic Flood of 1903.* Washington, D.C.: Dept. of the Interior, U.S. Geological Survey, Hydrographic Branch, 1903.

Leuchtenburg, William E. *Franklin D. Roosevelt and the New Deal.* New York: Harper and Row, 1963.

Linn, William Alexander. "Slavery in Bergen County, New Jersey." *Papers and Proceedings of the Bergen County Historical Society.* 4 (1907-08), 23-40.

Livingston, Rosa Ackerman. *Ackerman Homesteads: A Saga of Ackerman Lives and Times.* Waldwick, N.J.: Waldwick Publishing Co., 1983.

Lossing, Benson J. *The Pictorial Field-Book of the Revolution.* New York: Harper, 1859. Vol. 1.

Lucey, Carol S. *The Geology of Bergen County in Brief.* Trenton: Bureau of Geology and Topography, 1971.

McMahon, Reginald. "Liberty Pole: A Report on the Historic Site at Englewood, N.J." *Bergen County History* (1977), 113-132.

_____. "Vriessendael: A Note." *New Jersey History.* 87, (1969). 173-180.

Mack, Arthur C. *The Palisades of the Hudson.* Edgewater, N.J.: Palisades Press, 1909.

Mola, Geraldine. *We've Come a Long Way.* [East Paterson, N.J.]: East Paterson Republican Campaign Committee, 1972.

Mosley, Virginia T. *Tenafly: 1894-1969.* Tenafly, N.J.: Tenafly 75th Jubilee Committee, 1969.

_____. *Tenafly School Names.* Tenafly, N.J.: Mosley, [1973?]

Muller, Peter O. "Everyday Life in Suburbia: A Review of Changing Social and Economic Forces That Shape Daily Rhythms Within the Outer City." *American Quarterly.* (1982), 262-277.

Mumford, Lewis. *The City in History.* New York: Harcourt, Brace & World, 1961.

New Jersey State Federation of Women's Clubs. *A History of the New Jersey State Federation of Women's Clubs, 1894-1958.* n.p.: The Federation, 1958.

Newark Sunday Call. *Motor Highways of New Jersey.* Newark, N.J., 1918.

Norris, Herbert and Curtis, Oswald. *Costume and Fashion: The Nineteenth Century.* London: J. M. Kent, 1933. Vol. 6.

The Old Guard: A Monthly Journal Devoted to the Principles of 1776 and 1787. Ed. C. Chauncey Burr. New York: Van Evrie, Horton & Co., 1864, Vol. 2.

[Owen, Lewis]. *The Ackerman-Zabriskie-Steuben House.* River Edge, N.J.: Bergen County Historical Society, [1976?].

"The Packer Industries in Saddle River." *Heritage News,* (April 1980).

Passaic and Rutherford and Their Points of Interest. New York: Commercial Publishing Company, 1895.

Passaic River Flood District Commission (N.J.). *Report of the Passaic River Flood District Commission,* Dec. 1, 1906. [Paterson, N.J.]: Paterson Chronicle Co., 1907.

Phyfe, Helen McCulloch. *The Haworth Story.* Haworth, N.J., Frederick W. Schmidt, 1956.

Ransom. James M. "The Undercliff Settlements." *Bergen County History* (1974), [52]-69.

Read, D. D., ed. *The Bergen County Democrat's History of Hackensack, N.J.* Hackensack, N.J.: Bergen County Democrat, 1898.

Records of the Reformed Dutch Churches of Hackensack and Schraalenburgh, N.J. New York: Holland Society of New York, 1891. Part II.

Reeve, Arthur. *Demarest: Its People and History.* [Demarest, N.J.: Demarest Tercentenary Committee?], 1964.

Reilly, H. V. Pat. *A Pictorial History of Teterboro Airport, 1918 to 1976.* Teterboro, N.J.: Teterboro Aviation Hall of Fame, [1976?].

Ridgewood, N.J. Citizens Semi-Centennial Association, 1916. *Ridgewood, Bergen County, New Jersey.* Ridgewood: The Association, 1916.

Ridgewood State Tercentenary Committee. History Committee. *The History of a Village: Ridgewood, N.J.* Ridgewood: Village of Ridgewood, 1964.

Riesman, David. *The Lonely Crowd,* New Haven: Yale Univ. Press, 1950.

Riis, Jacob A. *How the Other Half Lives.* New York: Scribner & Sons, 1890.

Robertson, James Oliver. *American Myth, American Reality.* New York: Hill & Wang, 1980.

Ronald Zweig Associates. *A Study of Health Services Provided by Bergen County.* Hackensack, 1979.

Schmidt, Hubert G. *Agriculture in New Jersey: A Three Hundred Year History.* New Brunswick, N.J.: Rutgers University Press, 1973.

Scott, William W. *History of Passaic and Its Environs:* New York: Lewis Historical Publishing Co. 1922. 3 Vols.

Shanks, David C. *As they Passed Through the Port.* Washington, D.C.: Cary Pub. Co., 1927.

Sills, Yole, et al. *A College Comes of Age: Ramapo College of New Jersey, 1969-1977.* [Mahwah, N.J.: The College, 1977].

Sisson, Eva Browning. *The Story of Tenafly.* [Tenafly, N.J.]: Tenafly Trust Co., 1939.

Smeltzer, Chester A. *The Birth of Ramsey;* and Dater, John Y. *The Growth of Ramsey.* [Ramsey, N.J.]: Ramsey Journal Print, 1949.

Smith, Leon. ed. *The Story of New Milford, New Jersey: Birthplace of Bergen County.* [New Milford, N.J.]: Borough of New Milford, 1964.

Smith, J. Spencer. "The Locating of Camp Merritt." *Eighteenth Annual Report of the Bergen County Historical Society,* 13, (1920), 52-54.

Souvenir and Programme, Grand Opening Fair of the Union Club of Rutherford, New Jersey. [Rutherford]: The Union Club, [1892].

Spehr, Paul C. *The Movies Begin: Making Movies in New Jersey 1887-1920.* Newark, N.J.: Newark Museum, 1977.

Stebbins, Theodore E. *The Life and Works of Martin Joseph Heade.* New Haven: Yale University Press, 1975.

Sterling, Adaline W. *The Book of Englewood.* Englewood: City of Englewood, 1922.

Swartwout, John and Peters, Richard. "On Salt Marsh." *Memoirs of the Philadelphia Society for Promoting Agriculture,* 5 (1818), 248-285.

Tanner, Edwin P. *The Province of New Jersey, 1664-1738.* New York: AMS Press, 1967.

Taylor, Mildred. *The History of Teaneck.* [Teaneck, N.J.]: Teaneck American Revolution Bicentennial Committee, 1977.

Tholl, Claire K. "A Guide to the Whereabouts of Washington During the War for Independence (Bergen and Surrounding Counties)." *Bergen County History,* (1974) 71-99.

_____. "Preservation in Bergen." *Bergen County History* (1973) 63-[95].

Troy, Leo. *Organized Labor in New Jersey.* Princeton: Van Nostrand, 1965.

Vallario, Susan Anisfield. "Something for Everyone: The Hackensack Meadowlands Environment Center." *Meadowlands USA,* 7 (June 1982), 28-32.

Vermeule, Cornelius Clarkson. "The Floods of October, 1903: Passaic Floods and Their Control." *Annual Report of the State Geologist for the Year 1903.* Trenton: MacCrellish & Quigley, 1904.

Vervaet, Ryerson. *The Valley of Homes: The Ponds, Yaupough, Oakland, 1695-1952.* Oakland, N.J.: printed for the Fiftieth Anniversary Committee, 1952.

Volyn, Robert Paul. *The Broad Silk Industry in Paterson, New Jersey: A Troubled Industry in Microcosm, 1920 Through 1935.* Ph.D. Dissertation, N.Y.U. 1980.

Walker, A. H. *Atlas of Bergen County, New Jersey.* Reading, Pa.: C.C. Pease, 1876.

Warner, Sam Bass. *Streetcar Suburb: The Process of Growth in Boston, 1870-1900.* Cambridge, Mass.: Harvard Univ. Press, 1962.

Wendehack, Clifford C. *Early Dutch Houses of New Jersey: An Architectural Monograph.* White Pine Monograph Series, No. 61, ed. Russell F. Whitehead, New York, 1925.

West, Roscoe L. *Elementary Education in New Jersey: A History.* Princeton: Van Nostrand, 1964.

Westervelt, Francis A. "The Final Century of the Wampum Industry in Bergen County New Jersey." *Papers and Proceedings of the Bergen County Historical Society.* 12 (1916-17), [20]-38.

_____. "Hackensack Township, Bergen County, Province of East New Jersey, 1693: Facts and Figures from Eight Hundred Manuscripts." *Papers and Proceedings of the Bergen County Historical Society.* 11 (1915/16), 62.

_____. ed. *History of Bergen County, New Jersey, 1630-1923.* New York: Lewis Historical Publishing Co., 1923. 3 vols.

Whiffen, Marcus. *American Architecture Since 1780: A Guide to the Styles,* Cambridge, Mass: MIT Press, 1969.

Wiebe, Robert H. *The Search For Order, 1877-1920.* New York: Hill & Wang, 1967.

Wilkie, David J. *Esquire's American Autos and Their Makers.* New York: Esquire Inc., 1963.

Woodward, Henry P. *Copper Mines and Mining in New Jersey.* Geologic Series, No. 57. Trenton: New Jersey Department of Conservation and Development, 1944.

Works Projects Administration (N.J.). Writers' Program. *Bergen County Panorama.* Hackensack, N.J.: Bergen County Board of Chosen Freeholders, 1941.

About the Authors

For the past twenty years Catharine Fogarty has been the librarian in charge of the New Jersey Room Collection at Fairleigh Dickinson University's Messler Library in Rutherford, building its fine collection from a few bookstacks to over 10,000 books, documents, maps and manuscripts. She is a charter member and a past president of the History and Bibliography Section of the New Jersey Library Association and serves on the New Jersey State Historical Records Advisory Board.

John E. O'Connor is professor of History at New Jersey Institute of Technology. He holds a Ph.D. in American History from the City University of New York and is the author/editor of five books. His work on the use of visual resources for the research and teaching of history has been supported by grants from the Rockefeller Foundation and the National Endowment for the Humanities. Currently he is director of a related project for the American Historical Association and the editor of the journal *Film & History*.

Charles Cummings is Supervising Librarian of the New Jersey Reference Division of the Newark Public Library. He has authored, co-authored and edited articles, indexes and books including the Stevens Family Papers at the New Jersey Historical Society, The *Star Ledger* Index, and, with John O'Connor, *The New Jersey Television News Index and Abstracts,* and *Newark: An American City* (1979). He is a fellow of the New Jersey Historical Society.